Falling into
JOY

Eight simple steps to allow your body to become your best friend.

Conni Ponturo

BALBOA.
PRESS

A DIVISION OF HAY HOUSE

Balboa Press books may be ordered through booksellers or by contacting:

Balboa Press
A Division of Hay House
1663 Liberty Drive
Bloomington, IN 47403
www.balboapress.com
1 (877) 407-4847

Because of the dynamic nature of the Internet, any web addresses or
links contained in this book may have changed since publication and
may no longer be valid. The views expressed in this work are solely those
of the author and do not necessarily reflect the views of the publisher,
and the publisher hereby disclaims any responsibility for them.

The author of this book does not dispense medical advice or prescribe
the use of any technique as a form of treatment for physical, emotional,
or medical problems without the advice of a physician, either directly
or indirectly. The intent of the author is only to offer information
of a general nature to help you in your quest for emotional and
spiritual well-being. In the event you use any of the information in
this book for yourself, which is your constitutional right, the author
and the publisher assume no responsibility for your actions.

Any people depicted in stock imagery provided by Thinkstock are
models, and such images are being used for illustrative purposes only.
Certain stock imagery © Thinkstock.

Print information available on the last page.

ISBN: 978-1-5043-7681-5 (sc)
ISBN: 978-1-5043-7682-2 (e)

Library of Congress Control Number: 2017903872

Balboa Press rev. date: 04/18/2017

This book is dedicated to my husband, Don, who has given me so much unexpected joy, and to my children, Joey and Hannah, the joys of my life.

It's rare to find a book that creates a creative space for transformation, countless insights and sheer joy. *Falling into Joy* is that book. It's profoundly simple and highly practical. And, it's delightfully inspiring. Through many illustrative stories and entertaining narratives, you'll begin to redefine joy. The methods you'll learn work. And the specific techniques teach you ways to master the state of joy so that you can easily bring more of it into your life – feeling good physically, balanced emotionally and connected spiritually – laying the foundation to live more fully and gaining the momentum to achieve greater happiness.

Marsh Engle, Founder of The One Million Called, Author of *The Sacred Agreements and the AMAZING WOMAN multi-book series.*

www.marshengle.com

This book is for all of you who deserve unbridled joy in your lives. To feel alive in your bodies and souls. To know that every day is a gift to be cherished and acknowledged. To pay attention to the joys in your lives and not let them pass you by. Notice the little joys in your lives, and they will lead you to more joys. Live in gratitude because it will bring you more joy. My wish is that this book helps you achieve all of this. Nothing is ever wasted.

Disclaimer

The information contained in this book is intended to provide helpful and informative material on the above subject. It is not intended to serve as a replacement for professional medical advice. Any use of the information in this book is at the reader's discretion. The author and publisher specifically disclaim any and all liability arising directly or indirectly from the use or application of any information contained in this book. A health care professional should be consulted regarding any specific situation.`

Contents

Preface

I grew up the youngest and only girl in my family of six—three older brothers, my mother, and my father. We lived in Glen Cove, Long Island, a beautiful place in which to grow up and then run away from because I wanted the big city. I left Long Island at seventeen, only to return for quick visits, and moved into New York City with all of my dreams packed up in my dancing future. I was a mover, a dancer—always had been. So off I went to New York University Tisch School of the Arts.

It was magical the first two years, but then at the end of my sophomore year, the entire faculty changed over, and I felt lost. I started having searing pain in my feet. It became increasingly harder to walk, let alone dance. I saw a top orthopedic doctor. He said I had osteoarthritis and the bones of a sixty-year-old woman at nineteen. His prescription for me was to stop dancing. The pain and difficulty that caused was overwhelming. My whole identity was tied up with dancing, performing, and my body. If I wasn't a dancer, then who was I? I dropped out of college and stopped dancing—both things I thought I would never do.

I was missing joy. I was searching for my life. What would my new life be? I started working with a massage therapist for my headaches, which I'd had since I was a young teenager. Unable to express my emotions very well, my frustrations came out as headaches. As we worked on my head and I tried different relaxation techniques and started therapy, I began to experience fewer and fewer headaches. My therapist thought I would be good at massage, so I started training to become a massage therapist.

I worked with dancers because I knew what hurt their bodies and what exercises they would need to keep their bodies supple and strong. It seemed like a perfect transition for me. I worked with dancers on Broadway and in small companies, but I missed performing. I knew I couldn't dance anymore, but I had taken an acting class in college. Even though I was terrified of being that exposed, I loved how it pushed me. I found a fantastic class with William Alderson from the Neighborhood Playhouse. He taught the Sanford Meisner technique, which stressed learning to live in the moment as an actor and letting go of any idea of result. He is an amazing teacher, and he led all of our first- and second-year classes into incredible growth. I found my best friend, Anne, in that class, and we have remained friends for more than thirty years. All of the other students were young, talented, and full of hope for working in show business. I wonder what happened to all of them. After we finished our classes, I found a manager and started doing commercials. I was well on my way to doing what I loved to do.

I was looking for love and connection. And I wanted to be married and have children because I was getting older. I had a tumultuous, short first marriage, and I was moving into my mid-thirties and wondering if I would ever find love. I dated a lot and was always comfortable with men because I had three older brothers; men never scared or baffled me.

For the first time, I finally stopped worrying about what I didn't have and started enjoying my life more, having more fun and experiencing more joy. Then I found him. He had been close to me all along—a friend, someone expressing his talents through writing and patiently waiting for me. I finally picked up my head and noticed Don was the love of my life. He has been the perfect choice for more than twenty-five years, through hard times and fantastic times. He has been there for me and our family. I'm glad I followed my joy and allowed myself to see and trust him and love him.

We have two beautiful children, and both of us have grown and changed over the years. It was after my daughter was one and a half that I started feeling like I wanted more in my life. I had a deep longing to be of service in some way. I loved having children and had waited a long time to have them, but I knew I needed to be more in the world. I didn't even know what that meant at the time. I felt very alone in it all and also guilty for feeling like motherhood was not enough for me, especially after trying for a while to get pregnant and wanting it so badly.

Around that time, I was taking a movement class for new moms. A friend of mine knew I had taught aerobics when I was in college and asked me if I could teach the class for a while so she could finish a project she had been working on. I started teaching and didn't realize I was teaching Pilates mat classes. I loved it and had found my home. I looked in the mirror as I was teaching, and it all became crystal clear: I was happy—deep in my soul and bones happy. This is what I was meant to do. Coincidentally, my husband came home one day and told me about an article he'd read about Pilates and said he thought it would be perfect for me. I started to search for a teacher and found the perfect one, who ultimately became my mentor and friend.

But how was I going to do it all: young kids, financial commitment, and time commitment? It all seemed overwhelming at the time. Yet, it all seemed to fall into place somehow. My husband took my children to school in the mornings, and I found someone to keep my daughter for a few hours after school till I got home. I went into Beverly Hills very early so I could get home in time to get the kids from school, and I was home in the afternoons studying for the next day. It was a crazy time but energizing and somewhat magical. I became the student I had always wanted to be in school. I woke up at five o'clock, before the kids were up, to study anatomy. I raised my hand all the time in class—something I had been afraid to do while I was in school. I wanted to participate so much that the teacher would say, "Anyone other than Conni?" I threw myself into every situation I could, and I always said yes.

Finally, I got up the nerve to ask for a job. That was the pivotal moment that sent me off into what I love to do. I was lucky enough to work and watch a brilliant teacher, Maria Leone of Bodyline Fitness, and that is where I developed my unique eye for movement and injury. I took the clients no one wanted—the annoying and difficult ones. I would try different ways of working with clients who had injury issues and found that I kept coming up with new ideas and ways to solve problems. I was up at five o'clock in the morning and out the door. It was a perfect situation for me, which led to my becoming a studio owner and working with hundreds of clients and changing their lives.

I had found my home and my connection to spirit. If you have ever done something that is creative, you understand that it moves you in a very special way. Gardening, writing, painting, acting, dancing, listening to music, scrapbooking, decorating, and teaching—just to name a few—all connect you to a larger version of yourself. They connect you to your inner spirit. You are letting your expression talk for you rather than your brain. That's why it is a soul connection. I could not let go of my feeling of being of service to others. I couldn't squelch the deep *yes* going on in my heart, so I followed it. At the end of that little voice was my *joy*! Lessen your grip on fear and come into your *yes*, whatever it is, and ultimately your *joy*!

We all have the ability to transform ourselves and our lives. Who are you yearning to become?

Don't be afraid to look back at your life and see where you have been—all the scary stuff and the stuff you don't want to admit to. It is all perfectly planned. As I started to write this, I wanted to crawl out of my skin. It all seemed trivial and stupid. Who cares about any of this or my life at all?

It was my husband, Don, who said: "Show people who you are and why joy is important to you so they can understand. People need to hear your pain and then your success."

This is my story. We are more alike than we are different. Take a step forward in your life. Be honest with yourself, but be kind and loving too. Treat yourself as you would treat a friend. You are your own best friend, so talk lovingly to yourself. Look backward so you can see your future. What you did right besides what went wrong. Our mistakes are the lessons from which we learn the most. Don't fear them so much. Take a chance and find out what you really need and allow the joy to fill your life. You might be living in joy and not even realize it. Breathe and allow all of it in because there is nothing more important than you.

Introduction

Joy Is the Juice of Life, Freshly Squeezed.

I believe joy is important for every single one of us. I believe that we all deserve joy. I believe we are all worthy of having joy. In my work, I am lucky enough to reach people on a physical level where they can begin to move their bodies and feel the pleasure of movement and, in time, joy. I don't tell people that's what I do, but it is. I teach Pilates, and I am lucky enough to love what I do. I get to work with fantastic people and have wonderful teachers at my studio. I am very lucky.

The vulnerability of the body is scary for all of us. This is even more true when it doesn't move the way we want it to or the way it used to, especially when that was twenty or more years ago. Most of the time, this is what I hear from my clients: "I don't like my body anymore!" "Why does my body move this way? It never used to." "I don't like it!" "I don't like anything about myself." "I'm fat." "Where did I get this belly?" And so forth. Rarely do we move our bodies with love and kindness. That's where I come in. It is my job to remind you of how perfect you are—right where you are! That's right, I said right where you are—with the pain, the fat, the inflexibility, the resistance to change—and it is all perfectly planned. This is why I show up in your life.

I want you to remember when you used to love the way you looked and moved. I want you to remember how you looked at yourself with sweetness and love—the same way we look at babies and ooh and ah over them. We don't yell at them for their cute little tummies and chubby thighs. We love their instability while they are working diligently on a new skill, and yet we are so unforgiving of ourselves, unsupportive and unloving to our bodies and our hearts. You can change your body, but only when you learn to respect and love yourself. Our bodies support us our entire lives, and we only really notice them when we are in pain or when they don't move the way they used to.

It is our job as humans to make our bodies the best they can be—to stand tall when gravity is pulling us down as we age or when sitting in front of the computer makes us unable to sit up straight. We need to counteract the aging process and strengthen our muscles and learn how to relax and stretch to counterbalance the effects of overworking and sitting too much. We need to feel the best in our bodies, and when we don't feel good, we need to listen and see where we have gone off course.

The alignment in our bodies is very important, and in time we can correct our movements, change our vision of the way we are supposed to be, and start to live from a new and stronger foundation—a foundation that is true for where we are right now.

Why now? Why the question of joy? Isn't joy really the dirty little secret that nobody wants to talk about? Isn't it the word everyone whispers? *Joy!* Oh really, you are feeling that? How come you have that and I don't? What does it mean to live in a body that has the opportunity for endless, unbridled joy? I can't believe you're even saying that! What does that even look like, or would we notice it if we saw it? There are lots of questions to answer.

Joy is so undervalued in our culture. The ability to find the nugget of deep happiness is so overlooked and looked down upon that it has become a secret word. It is so overused that no one feels it. It is so undervalued that no one will say it. *Wow.* How did we get here?

Let's go back to childhood, when playing together with a friend was all that mattered. Laughing and being silly and joyful was how we lived most of our days. Everything was silly and wondrous. The fiber that makes up most children is pure joy. As grown-ups we don't really like children. Yes, I am making a gross assumption, but think about it: all the yelling, playing, laughing, and craziness. We dislike it, and what we really prefer is when children are quiet. All the crazy energy from children makes us very uncomfortable, which is why we are always quieting them down. It brings up uncomfortable feelings that we have in our own bodies. "Stop it!" "Be quiet!" "Sit down." As if saying such things will quiet the joyful beast that lives in all of them. I remember when my children were small and wanting them to behave in public as if their behavior were an extension of me. Life makes us so serious; there's a lot to get done, and we need to get it done now, says the hurried adult.

The definition of *joy* in the dictionary is" 1a: the emotion evoked by well-being, success, or good fortune or by the prospect of possessing what one desires: Delight b: the expression or exhibition of such emotion: Gaiety 2: a state of happiness or felicity: Bliss 3: a source or cause of delight." (Merriam-Webster.com)

The concept behind the definitions of joy can bring discomfort and fear into our bodies—discomfort because those words feel foreign to us in the way we live and function in the world. We get stuck in the rut of our daily lives, and sometimes when we try to break free, it feels hard and uncomfortable. We feel disconnected from our jobs, our families, our communities, and finally ourselves. Why? Because we are always looking outside ourselves to find the answers. We often feel like other people have what we need, when we have had the answers we are searching for all along. If we start to listen to our inner voice, suddenly we start to see where we need to function from. We can see in that moment that that's where we need to live and allow the joy of who we really are to fill us. It can translate into our souls' mission and can ultimately take us to calm within our heart. Calm turns into peace, and then we allow our lives to move into joy. Have you ever been quiet somewhere special, not wanting to feel anything other than peace? In that moment of calm, a bird flies by, or you notice something you never saw before. In that moment—in that breath of the moment—that's where joy comes in.

The disconnect we feel in our lives comes from the shoulds that live inside us: I should be thinner, taller, prettier, smarter, richer, happier, married, not married, sexier, and on and on. We all know what we don't have; we can write lists and lists of our flaws. But if asked for a list of what we love about ourselves, we go all quiet. Maybe we have one or two ideas, but they definitely don't flow out of us like our faults do.

In this book I want you to think about your first perception of joy. Is this memory a good or a bad feeling? What's the underlying thing that keeps you from joy? What are the scientific findings about joy? What are you longing for? What are your habits and the patterns that are keeping you from joy? Do you have pain in your body, and if so, what can you do about it? I want you to think about whether you even value what joy brings into your life. Do you think it is silly, frivolous, stupid, annoying, or totally irrelevant?

I have divided the book into what I believe the eight steps of joy look like: The Denial, The Gift of Pain, The Fatal Error, The Excuse, Centered within Self, The Vision, The Gateway, and The Reveal.

Each of the chapters contains a case study with a client and then an exercise. All of the exercises are simple, and you can do most of them anywhere. You choose what resonates with you. Try one new exercise a week or a month. Just give yourself time, and allow yourself to learn something new. Only with practice do we get better at anything. Only by taking the time to do the exercises can we feel the effects. Make time for yourself, and if you can't choose which one to do first, then I say always start with the breath. I want you to think about your life and what changes would bring more joyous relationships and experiences into your life.

The tools that I have given you will help you notice and hopefully keep more joy in your life.

Most of all I want you to notice the subtle way we sabotage our joy and how to value the joy in everyday life.

I want you to notice it and embrace it. Let it fill your life and make it better.

To me, *Joy* is the juice of life freshly squeezed. How will you drink it in?

Chapter 1

The Denial

If You're Not Sure Where to Start, Always Start with the Breath

Our deepest fear is not that we are inadequate. Our deepest fear is that we are powerful beyond measure. It is our light, not our darkness that most frightens us. We ask ourselves, who am I to be brilliant, gorgeous, talented, and fabulous? Actually, who are you not to be? You are a child of God. Your playing small does not serve the world. There is nothing enlightening about shrinking so that other people won't feel insecure around you. We were all meant to shine, as children do. We were meant to manifest the glory of God within us. It is not just in some of us but in all of us. And as we shine our own light, we unconsciously

1

give other people permission to do the same. As we are liberated from our own fear, our presence automatically liberates others (Williamson, 1992, pp.190–191).

I have always loved this passage by Marianne Williamson because it is true. Isn't it? We really don't fear failure as much as rising to the top. What will that mean to the people around us? Will we lose them? What if they don't like us anymore? What if they think we are stuck up? Then what?

We are unhappy because we are longing for quiet, a sense of being grounded, optimistic, open and free energy in our bodies, openheartedness, and in time, peace. But we have had those things all along, just as Dorothy did in *The Wizard of Oz*. The good witch says, "Just click your heels together and say, 'There's no place like home, no place like home.'" We have always been there, so all we need to do is open up our eyes and hearts and look around at what we have created.

Sometimes there is a payoff in living in failure. You don't need to try. You already know the outcome. *It is easier to be depressed than it is to be dynamic!* We need to push beyond the disappointments we feel about ourselves. Not following through is letting yourself down. That is much easier than pushing through and putting the pedal to the metal, so to speak, and just getting it done. It is fear that stops us. I understand that, and I have let myself down on many occasions, only to feel very disappointed in myself. We have trouble letting others down, but how many times in our lives have we let down the most important person—ourselves? We don't seem to value the *us* in our lives. Being called selfish is something we are so afraid of. Were we taught somewhere that self is not important? Selfishness is really self-love. I fight every day to keep myself in the forefront of my life. Not because I am so narcissistic, but rather because I allow everyone to move to the front of my life. The calls I need to make, errands, teaching, stuff for my family, and on and on, take precedence over sitting down and doing things for *me*. Carving out time to exercise, meet with friends, sit alone and just ponder nothing, take a bath, and go out in nature all get moved to one day on my bucket list. Doing just any one of those things feels better in our bodies and hearts.

Why are we so unhappy if we have everything we need?

Ultimately we want to be good, don't you think? We want to please everyone and make them like us and do well in our jobs. I don't know if men feel this, but most women do: the feeling of needing to be good and right. We want to answer the questions right. We want to be good girls and have everything turn out right in our lives—and have happily ever afters. I see it every day when we won't let ourselves be in the center of our own lives. Everyone else gets a piece of us, so we end up too tired to work out or take time to notice how our bodies are feeling. We are all intuitive; we just need to listen. If you are someone who has never really listened to that little voice inside, it will be quiet at first. If you stick with it and trust it, it will get louder and truer and truer over time.

There is a science behind the joy of sharing joy. In *Psychology Today*, Emma Seppälä, PhD says, "Positive experiences happen to us every day yet, we don't take full advantage of them." She goes on to ask:

> Ever notice that it has been a great day and you got eight hours of sleep, it's the weekend and you just spent quality time with a friend but it takes one harsh word from someone or one piece of bad news to ruin the day? (Seppälä 2013)

Research by Shelley Gable and Jonathan Haidt suggests that we actually have three times more positive experiences than negative ones. What makes us a slave to the bad feeling? Why do those experiences rate higher than our positive ones? ("What (and Why) is Positive Psychology" - "Review of General Psychology" 2005)

Researchers have identified two main tendencies that keep us from expanding, extending, and experiencing our joy: the negative bias and habituation. The negative bias refers to the mind's innate tendency to give more value to the negative, and habituation refers to the fact that while we receive boosts of happiness from new, positive experiences, over time we get used to these experiences and they no longer have the same effect.

I don't think we value our joys enough in this culture. When I started talking to people about what I wanted to do, I received many a blank stare, followed by, "Really? You're writing about that?" Yet, I feel it is so important to notice the joy all around us—to be open to others and allow both the good and the bad feelings of the day to wash through us, to acknowledge them but not to get too attached to either of them. If we can ride the waves of those feelings, in the end we can pick which one we want to land on. The most important point here, beyond all else, is that it starts with the breath and the ability to inhale and exhale, let go, and be present.

Tanya's story:

Tanya was a woman in her mid-fifties who was very unhappy in her life and in her body. She was about forty pounds overweight, and everything weighed her down. She ate too much and drank too much wine.

She had pain in her body, and she was ready to give up. She was negative all the time, and to be totally honest, I don't even know if I liked her at times. She showed up at my studio and wanted help. I asked what she wanted to change about her life, to which she answered, "Everything." That's a nice jumping-off point for me. When people are ready to strip away at the layer that makes them resist everything, then they are ready to begin to move beyond the physical side of what is holding them back. That's a start! We started moving a little at a time and doing a lot of deep breathing.

Breathing to me is essential; it connects us to the deepest part of ourselves and helps us focus inward.

Most of the time, we don't notice our breath. Our breathing is unconscious, and when we allow ourselves to focus on it, we become more centered. We need that, especially when we rush through most of the day. I made Tanya put all her expectations on hold and just do the work. We didn't talk about her diet, because I wanted to make her a mover first. When she became a really great mover, she started to think about her day differently: how much she could move in a day, parking farther away at the mall, and adding ten more minutes of waking. She took the stairs, she wore a Fitbit to track her steps, and suddenly it all became a game. When she left herself alone, she was really good; when she got into her head, she overanalyzed everything and became extremely critical of herself. When you criticize everything, you become that negative, lower-vibe energy, which causes you to become stagnate. Staying positive puts us in a much higher vibrational place.

Months went by, and Tanya started thinking about her wine and her eating. We talked about very simple things, from cutting her portions down to ideas for snacking and then tracking her food.

When you write down what you eat in a day, you can see where the holes in your diet are and where you tend to go off course.

In Tanya's case, the weight slowly came off, and her life and her attitude started to lift. She was very funny, and her smile and humor came back. She was rarely negative and was extremely appreciative and even noticeably happier, which made her look years younger. Funny how that can happen. It all started with her breathing.

Let's try some focused breathing right now.

Step 1: Breathing

Go ahead and laugh. Breathing? First, most of us don't consciously breathe—ever. Second, it seems so simple.

You can do this almost anywhere. If you are somewhere safe, then close your eyes; if you are driving, eyes open, of course. Sit up straight in a chair, in the car, anywhere you have support. Have your spine feel long, and if you are in a chair, rest against the back for support. Take a deep breath in through your nose, hold the breath for two counts, and then slowly let it out through your mouth, as if you are blowing through a straw. Try this ten more times. Return to breathing normally and just notice.

Notice whatever is going on in you. You may think this is annoying, stupid, boring, or relaxing—every feeling is okay. Keeping your eyes closed, I want you to pay attention to the gentle rise and fall of your belly; do this for a few breaths. Next, feel the rise and fall of your chest. Think of your chest as an accordion, filling the lungs out sideways and then contracting, slowly allowing the air to fill your chest.

Just notice.

Take a deep breath in, hold for two counts, and slowly let it out. Repeat your breathing ten more times. Don't worry about the count; just breathe and notice how you are feeling. Just let your body release and stay present. Try this during your day—before you get out of bed in the morning, at the end of the day, or when you are feeling very tired. If you are very angry or frustrated, this helps because it slows your heart rate down. When it slows down your heart rate, everything in your body starts to relax. Your blood pressure will drop, and you will notice yourself getting quieter and a little more present in your body. This is great to do when you are really frustrated with kids, your job, and your life. Do this right before you are about to explode, and it can take your blood pressure way, way down and keep you a little saner. Practice this often and try to take two deep breaths before you leave your car, go into work, go home, or go out to the store. Allow yourself to become centered. Allow it to become your breath mediation. We are creating new habits, so you will need to practice often. Try it for twenty-one days and see if you don't feel different.

Remember, it all starts with the breath.

Recap Chapter 1

The Denial

1. It's time to become the center of your life.
2. Positive experiences happen to us every day, but we tend to focus on the negative ones.
3. What you think about becomes your life.
4. Breathe and develop focused breathing. Take a deep breath in for two counts, hold for two counts, and slowly exhale out through your mouth for two counts. Do it ten times.
5. Before you get out of bed, take two focused breaths, and again before going to work, picking up your kids, getting in your car, and going to bed. Let your deep breaths keep you in the moment.

Chapter 2

The Gift of Pain

Pain is a voice we need to listen to.

I am going to address the female population for a few moments to explain how women are different from men. As women, we are givers—at least most of us are—and yet, we are often very stingy with ourselves. I hear this day in and day out about how there isn't enough time and how we don't know how to help ourselves. I think we do know, but we deny ourselves out of self-loathing. We deny ourselves the very thing that we want, because then we would be whole. We would have no more excuses, and ultimately, we might be happier.

Let's think about that for a minute. Is that why it is so hard to attain our goals? Because we might get what we want, and that is the very thing we are afraid of? That means we are also afraid of the loss of the old us—the old definition of us that we hold everything we want at arm's length just to keep ourselves in the place that feels comfortable and safe. Afraid that if we stretch—and believe me, it is a stretch—and have some discomfort, we won't be able to handle it.

I have days when I give and I give and I give, and at the end of the day, I have very little left for myself. I am so disappointed with myself on those days. I am disappointed because I didn't go for a walk or sit outside and enjoy the birds or sit with a cup of tea or take a bath or call a friend. At those times I usually eat food I don't want to eat, drink too much wine, and fail to nurture myself. I am too *tired* to nurture myself. Continue this year in and year out, and now the healer is compromised, the mother is compromised, the father is compromised, the worker is compromised, the student is compromised, the grandparent is compromised, and on and on. In that moment, I really feel as if I have let myself down, and I have, because everyone and everything goes to the top of my list. The flip side of this is that when I do one thing that really takes care of me, I feel good, and on most days, I feel great! I end my day satisfied that I helped others, yet I also took care of the most important person, which is me. Self-care has got to go to the top of our list of things to do in the day.

Whenever I have clients who tell me they are in pain, I tell them that's their gift. Of course, I get a totally confused look until what I am saying begins to make sense to them. The body is always talking to you and asking you to listen. Most times we don't listen unless we are in pain. I think I heard Oprah say it: "First, life throws you a pebble, and if you don't get that, it throws a brick, and if you don't get that, it throws a boulder, and if you don't get that, you hit a brick wall." Something to wake us up, so we finally get the message. When we feel good in our bodies and all is right, we don't think about our bodies. Only when there is a problem that hurts enough do we make a change. We will do anything to get out of pain. That's when I get the most calls. Help, I need to see you right now!

How can we change that?

What is it we really want but cannot let ourselves have? Peace. I feel it is peace in our souls. In all the hectic craziness around us, I think in our hearts, we want some sort of peace, unconditional love, and understanding from ourselves—as if we are our own best friends. We are, and yet we forget ourselves. We leave us out of the party. We deny ourselves the very things we really want from our best friends: connection and compassion.

What does peace feel like? A description in Merriam-Webster Dictionary.com is 1: a state of tranquility or quiet: such as a: freedom from civil disturbance b: a state of security or order within a community provided for by law or custom. 2. freedom from disquieting or oppressive thoughts or emotions. (Merriam-Webster.com) Can you image what that would mean in your life and your body? Have you ever been in that place? Even for a split second? I would venture to say yes, you have been there, but the number of times has been few and far between, because it is often out of your comfort range. But that is where we need to live: out of our comfort range, so the new place—that expanded space—becomes comfortable. Does the feeling of needing perfection in our lives keep us from getting close to our truth? The answer to that is *yes*! Because things will never be good enough. That feeling of never being good enough because we are not perfect lives deep inside of all of us. But how can that be when we are all magnificent beings just by being alive?

What if we start off each day with what I call *me* focus: What am I going to do for myself today?

Do one thing a day that takes care of your soul, and you will notice it. That is the important part—that you notice for yourself, that you realize you are honoring your importance. Keep it small: have a cup of tea instead of running to do an errand, walk in the park, sit in nature, take a class you've been wanting to take, write a note to a friend, write a note to yourself, run or walk (especially when you don't want to), make yourself move in some way. It is in these smaller moments when we feel our hearts, so that when we give to others, we don't totally run out of steam for ourselves, and in those small moments, we find peace. Our posture is a physical representation of how we feel about ourselves and the way we perceive the world around us. Fear contracts the body, and joy expands the body. Anger rises to the top of the body and then explodes forward, outward. Shock freezes the body, and depression stops all movement in any direction. Stand tall and feel ready to take on the world.

Jay's story:

Jay was an overweight man in his early sixties—250 pounds and very unhappy. He was on ten medications, was prediabetic, and had high blood pressure, high cholesterol, pain in his knees that kept him from walking, and a bad back. What motivated him was his intense pain. He told me he would lie in bed afraid to turn over because his shoulder hurt, his knees hurt, and his back hurt. But his pain of living in his body was great, so any movement forward had to be better; he had hit his bottom, and the only way was up. He began his personal journey.

The hero's journey:

Joseph Campbell was an American mythologist, writer and lecturer, best known for his work in comparative mythology and comparative religion. He says the hero's journey begins when he receives a call to action, such as a direct threat to his safety. At this point, the hero refuses the call. He knows he must do it, and he has many fears about being able to complete the task, many self-doubts and second thoughts about the challenge. Then he meets a mentor, someone who believes in him and gives him wise advice and the tools for his adventure. Now ready, the hero can begin his quest. He will be pushed beyond his comfort level. He will cross from a world that he is familiar with to one that is unknown, and he must decide that he alone can survive, overcome any obstacles, and become victorious. Is embarking on the journey of losing one hundred pounds any different than slaying dragons? I don't think so.

Two things really helped Jay on his hero's adventure: First, he had been active when he was younger, and second, he was a concert violinist, and he understood discipline. He knew that he had to do the work, and no one was going to do it for him. He was in control of his eating, cooked healthy food for himself, and made sure that he exercised. He was ready to put himself back into the center of his life.

We started very slowly (because he couldn't go any faster), walking five minutes one way and then turning around and walking five minutes back. That's all he could do without going into pain. Within weeks he was up to ten, then fifteen minutes. We also started talking about food differently, eating smaller portions and having six small meals a day, just focusing on losing one pound at a time. That was it; thinking about one hundred pounds was too overwhelming, but one pound at a time was doable.

During the next couple of months, his waist size changed, his ability to walk for longer periods of time increased, and he experienced less pain. We did Pilates and worked on stabilizing and strengthening his deep back muscles and his abdominals and stretching two times a week. The work was slow, but he was changing quickly. His food portions grew smaller, and he cut out unhealthy foods. He was a good cook, so he ate more food at home and less at restaurants. He started to experiment with cooking healthy and interesting food. That way he could control his environment and the food that went into his body.

He was getting stronger and feeling and looking good. His back pain was gone, and as he lost the weight, his knee pain lessened as well. He had plateaus within the year, but he knew how to refocus his eating, or we would change our workouts if we needed to. He added intervals to his walking and was focused on his end goal.

It took him a year to lose one hundred pounds. Every time I think about him, I am amazed and can barely remember that man who had walked into my studio one year earlier. Now he is vibrant, looking wonderful, and working more because he looks younger, and he can handle any stress in his body. It is as if the clock went backward in time. After the first year, his next challenge was maintaining his weight loss. Now, many years later, he is still maintaining his weight loss and looking and feeling terrific. Even with setbacks—and he has had a few—he gets back on his moving schedule and gets back to eating right. His health improves because he pays attention, and unlike before, it is important to him. He makes time for it and values himself.

Jay's testimony:

I weighed more than at any time in my entire life and was in constant pain. I'm sixty-two, and my blood pressure, cholesterol, and stress levels were all in the critical danger zone. I decided I'd had enough. I joined Absolute Pilates Upstairs and made a commitment to myself to change my life, and I have. I have successfully utilized twice a week personal Pilates training, walking, and Conni's excellent real-word dietary and teaching expertise to dramatically improve my life.

As of today, July 20, 2010, (four and a half months later), I have lost forty-five pounds. I feel better, my chronic back pain is 80 percent better, I look better, and I am stronger and more flexible than I have been in years.

This is just the beginning. I no longer take any blood pressure meds or back pain meds, and my cholesterol is 125 points lower.

Conni and her first-rate teachers are first class, compassionate, and caring.

Step 2: Walking Meditation

To me, walking is one of the best exercises. You can do it anywhere, no cost involved. You can go to beautiful areas where you can work out creative ideas you have in your mind or argue out loud with the trees. You can rid yourself of your daily angst in the world. I want you to think differently about exercise. How can you bring it into your daily life so you are more active in the day? One way is to park farther away from the entrance to the mall or the grocery store, post office, or anywhere else you plan on running your errands. After a dinner at a restaurant, go for a walk around the block a couple of times before you go back to your car to add more steps in your day. Get up every hour from your desk and move to add movement and steps to your day. And clear your head in the afternoon by taking a walking break instead of a coffee break during which you may be tempted to eat junk food.

I want you to challenge yourself by getting a pedometer, Fitbit, Apple watch, or Jawbone UP and try to get in ten thousand steps a day. If you are seventy or older, eight thousand a day is the recommendation. If you are totally deconditioned, start slowly and start small, walking five minutes one way and five minutes back. As you get stronger, go up to twenty minutes. Keep adding minutes slowly and try to get up to sixty. Remember to park at the back of the parking lot. Two things will happen: First, by parking farther away, you will always find a space. And, second, you will get your steps in.

Walking meditation:

I want you to think of your walk as a meditation. That means you are spending time with yourself and focusing on you. I like to exercise early in the morning. If you are not a morning person, find a time that works for you, but stick to it. Don't let your procrastination get the better of you. Start walking, taking five small breaths in through your nose and five small breaths out through your mouth as you walk. In Pilates there is an exercise called the Hundred, and it is called that because you take in five small breaths through your nose and five breaths out through your mouth for ten rounds, making it one hundred breaths. The purpose of the Hundred is to wake up the body and get the heart, lungs, and the rest of the body warmed up.

Let's use the Hundred breathing in your walk. Remember: Take five small breaths in through your nose and five small breaths out through your mouth as you walk. Start out with your breath in sync with your steps—breath for breath, step for step. Easy does it. Keep it slow and steady. Don't force any feeling or outcome. Always stop if you feel funny in any way or can't catch your breath. Take yourself out to the park (or find a treadmill); before you start walking, center yourself. Close your eyes and take a deep breath in and slowly let it out. Now open your eyes and look at where you are. I mean really look around at the trees, the mountains, the ocean, or just up at the sky, whatever space you are in. Take in the beauty that is always around you that you often fail to take it in.

Now start your walk with an easy step. Take in your surroundings and just notice. Keep your breathing easy. Think of this as a walking meditation instead of merely going around the block mindlessly or walking or running on the treadmill without thought. I want you to honor yourself and value your time. Look at everything around you and let your thoughts flow in and just flow out. No judgments to anything. Just move and let your thoughts move through you. Make a game out of it and challenge yourself every day. You are trying to get to ten thousand steps; that is around five miles. Many of my clients go way beyond that, so challenge yourself. Find a friend and compete against one another or motivate each other to move every day.

After your walk, take a few minutes to breathe and center yourself. Notice how you feel. Give yourself the space. Don't run off to work, but be very present in your body. Maybe a few thoughts for your joy journal have come up—things to be thankful for. I will go into more detail later about your joy journal, this is where you want to write down all the fantastic joy around you. Everything you can envision. Write them all down. Give yourself some credit for moving your body today. Give yourself the pat on the back that no one else is giving you. Go ahead and become your own cheerleader. Give yourself permission to be boastful about your progress, your body is listening.

Recap Chapter 2

The Gift of Pain

1. Why are we so stingy with ourselves? Is it because we might get what we really want if we let ourselves focus?

2. Your pain is your gift. That's how our bodies talk to us, through our feeling. Feeling great feels good and usually means we are in alignment, whereas feeling bad or in pain means we have gone off course somewhere and need to refocus and listen to our bodies.

3. Daily *me* focus: What do I really need in this moment? Asking that question and listening to the answer is key for us to live in the moment. Have a cup of tea instead of running out to the mall. Journal and spend time listening to what your body needs instead of watching television. Connect with a friend instead of scrolling on Facebook. Get a massage and take care of your body instead of mindlessly eating sweets. Go outside and take a walk in nature, listen to your inner voice.

4. Walking meditation: Take five breaths in through your nose and then five breaths out through your mouth. Continue the pattern as you walk step for step, breath for breath.

5. Add walking to your daily life: Park farther away at the mall, at the supermarket, and at work. After dinner, go for a walk with your family. Make moving part of your life, and make taking extra steps a game.

Chapter 3

The Fatal Error

The fatal error is that we believe we are not enough.

When is it time to walk away?

I have struggled with this in my life. I left college after my sophomore year because I felt I wasn't being challenged. My foot was in pain, and I had lost my way. It pains me to say that, but staying for another two years seemed overwhelming to me. The entire dance department reorganized, and all my beloved teachers were leaving; I was unsure of the future of our department. Oh, and one more thing: I was in pain, and the answer the doctor gave me was to stop dancing. I walked away. No one could convince me otherwise. I was headstrong and thought I had all the answers. Why did I do that? What was I afraid of? Or did that send me off in a new direction to find a deeper me—the one I was supposed to become? I left acting; after ten years, I couldn't push through anymore.

I wasn't getting the calls or booking quite as much. I was always too young or too old for the part, and I was tired. It did not feel good in my soul anymore.

I walked away from that into what I love more than anything. What I learned in both my dancing and my acting practice I use every day. Those skills go into my life toolbox. We all have one. That's where we go when we need to dig deep and find a solution to a problem.

What have you walked away from? What were you afraid of? And why? Did you walk away because you feared that if you stayed with it you might succeed? Or maybe it was because it wasn't your path anymore and something new would arise from walking down another road and making a different choice. That's our fatal error: We judge the circumstance as good or bad, but maybe it was just time for something different. I used to feel so ashamed of the paths and places that I left, but I realize now those decisions have made up the fabric of who I am.

Choosing that different path has made me more compassionate to others when they struggle, because I have been there myself. It has helped me explain to students that staying in college is a better choice than leaving. I understood all the feelings they had about wanting to leave school, but I could see the bigger picture; it made me appreciate what I am able to do now, not what I can no longer do. I am a teacher who works with clients on their bodies, and I can't always find time to take care of my body. I am always chasing that last ten pounds. I know that in teaching and in writing, the audience I speak to is me. I am writing to my soul, so it can listen and know that beyond all else it is valued by me and loved. That is all we ever want to feel: valued and loved beyond all else. After cancer, a death or loss, divorce or breakup, or serious injury, are we allowed to feel joy again? Can we love ourselves enough to move forward and allow our feelings to come though? When we are in the middle of turmoil, it seems like life will never be different.

In her book *Daring Greatly*, Dr. Brené Brown says that the three lessons she learned about joy came from people who have spent time in sorrow and darkness:

1. **Joy comes to us in moments – ordinary moments. We risk missing out on joy when we get too busy chasing down the extraordinary.** Scarcity culture may keep us afraid of living small, ordinary lives, but when you talk to people who have survived great losses, it is clear that joy is a constant. Without exception, all of the participants who spoke to me about their losses, and what they missed the most, spoke of ordinary moments. "If I could come downstairs and see my husband sitting at the table cursing at the newspaper..." "If I could hear my son giggling in the backyard..." "My Mom sent me the craziest texts – she never knew how to work her phone. I'd give anything to get one of those texts right now."

2. **Be grateful for what you have.** When I asked people who have survived tragedy how we can cultivate and show more compassion for people who are suffering, the answer is always the same: Don't shrink away from the joy of your child because I've lost mine. Don't take what you have for granted – celebrate it. Don't apologize for what you have. Be grateful for it and share your gratitude with others. Are your parents healthy? Be thrilled. Let them know how much they mean to you. *When you honor what you have, you're honoring what I've lost.*

3. **Don't squander joy.** We can't prepare for tragedy and loss. When we turn opportunity to feel joy into a test drive for despair, we actually diminish our resilience. Yes, softening into joy is uncomfortable. Yes, it's scary. Yes, it's vulnerable. *But every time we allow ourselves to lean into joy and we give in to those moments, we build resilience and hope.* The joy becomes part of who we are, and when bad things happen – and they do happen – we are stronger (Brown, 2012, pp. 125-26).

Time is the great equalizer of life, am I right? So much changes in time: We age, we slow down, and we lose friends and loved ones. Yet, in the process, we grow into something different. A more thoughtful being? Maybe we don't take as much for granted. We cherish our friendships and family more. Can we tolerate imperfection in ourselves and others? It is not the twenty-year-old looking back at you in the mirror. You can't jump as high or run as fast or dance all night. But so what! Can you change that preset in your brain and just fall in love with the magnificent being staring back at you in the mirror? Can you fall in love with that older, wiser face? That's the place we all want to grow into.

Day in and day out I see my clients not finding the time to do this or walking away right before a huge breakthrough.

Fear is the force that stops us.

We are always one step away from whatever we want. We are often the ones who place the obstacles in our way. Can we start to move them away one by one and keep pushing forward to attain what we struggled to achieve for so long?

If we can start with one thing to bring about change in our lives, it should be our posture. Belle Beth Cooper talks about this in her article "The Science behind Posture and How It Affects Your Brain." In the article Cooper points out that the way we sit, stand, and walk has long-reaching implications on our moods and happiness. She relates that the Dutch behavioral scientist Erik Peper has done extensive research in this area. He regularly makes participants in his classes stand up and stretch because he believes that when we stand up straight, we are more likely to remember positive memories and to think of something positive in general. Another Peper insight

Cooper details is that if we skip during breaks (yes, that's right—skip), we can significantly increase our energy levels (Cooper, 2013). I wonder if that is why kids at recess in elementary school run and skip out to the playground. Maybe on our way to meetings instead of hurrying down the corridors we can train ourselves to skip; we might be more productive.

Amy Cuddy in her famous 2012 TED Talk has wonderful insight into how your body language shapes who you are. These are her words,

> So I want to start by offering you a free no-tech life hack, and all it requires of you is this: that you change your posture for two minutes. But before I give it away, I want to ask you to right now do a little audit of your body and what you're doing with your body. So how many of you are making yourselves smaller? Maybe you're hunching, crossing your legs, maybe wrapping your ankles. Sometimes we hold onto our arms like this. Sometimes we spread out. (Laughter) I see you. So I want you to pay attention to what you're doing right now. We're going to come back to that in a few minutes, and I'm hoping that if you learn to tweak this a little bit, it could significantly change the way your life unfolds.

Cuddy says, "If we can change our posture for two minutes a day we can change our life" (Cuddy, 2012).

When we cross our arms and legs, we retreat into ourselves, and when we take our arms behind our heads or open our arms up in victory, we expand. Cuddy says, "Sometimes we need to fake it till we make it and then in time the successful feeling becomes real" (Cuddy, 2012). The tiny tweaks that we make can have a big payoff. That is in only two minutes a day. We can step away from our desks and stand tall, take our arms behind our backs at hip level and clasp our fingers together and pull in our abdomens so we don't arch our backs; we can roll our shoulders back and down naturally and with ease and open ourselves up to a reconditioning of our posture—a posture that is tall and open in our chest.

Powerful people, celebrities, athletes, models, and royalty, just to name a few, have a strong sense of their bodies in space and of being larger than life or walking into a room with presence and charisma.

Does that mean there is no hope for the rest of us? No! It means you need to live in your body, being present and aware when you are not standing tall. This feeling that we live in our bodies—the feeling of presence—can change our brain chemistry. It is in the acting "as if" in our bodies that we start to change our reality. We can stand with our arms over our heads wide in a victory pose, before we give a talk, go for an interview, meet someone new, or do something that scares us, we can suddenly become a more powerful version of ourselves. Thank you Amy Cuddy.

Have you ever felt so excited by an idea, an event, or something special that you were waiting for and you actually felt four inches taller? That's what I mean. Are we really taller in our bodies? No and Yes, because we allow the muscles that run parallel to the spine to engage, and we stand taller. If we can give our bodies breaks throughout the day, we can give our brains a small vacation from all the stress also. We can begin to believe better stories about our life.

Try it.

Bruce's story:

This is where my next client comes in. When he first came to me, he couldn't stand tall. He was crouched over and in pain.

Bruce came into my studio fifteen years ago. He is the client I've had for the longest amount of time and a true joy. I admire everything about him, from the attention he gives to his business, to the time he takes to make sure his body works well. He is in a high-powered, stressful management position, but he knows if he doesn't take care of his body, he will really go downhill.

When he first came to see me, he had been referred through a friend. He was hunched over and couldn't get out of the chair without pushing up on his arms. He'd had two hip replacements, back issues, and arthritis. He was in pain and very stiff. He would say of himself, "I thought I was a disaster," but I thought of him as an exciting challenge. Our first order of business was to get him straighter in his body and to work on his mobility in his legs and spine. We would practice standing up from and sitting down into chairs, as well as discuss the correct way to get in and out of the car and how best to sit while in the office.

Over the years he got stronger and stronger and taller. He can now take care of himself when he experiences pain. There is no physical challenge that I can't throw his way. He is up for all of it: He does his stretching exercises at home; he plays golf, which he enjoys; and he has been very consistent about doing Pilates two times a week. The problems that he came to me with didn't totally disappear, but he learned over the years how to manage them and how to take care of his body. Other issues have shown up over the years, and he deals with them. We keep adding new exercises, and he continues to improve.

Bruce's testimony:

Pilates turned my life around. While that may sound like a hyperbole, it is true. Specifically, working with Conni Ponturo for the last fifteen years has turned my life around. Before I met Conni, I hurt all the time, I had difficulty getting out of a chair without assistance, and my lack of flexibility caused me to compensate in ways that affected my walking and posture.

While my arthritis continues to affect me, those effects have been greatly mitigated by my increased core strength and my markedly increased flexibility. The comments I have received regarding my improved appearance, demeanor, and overall well-being have been remarkable, particularly in that I've gotten older! At a recent fortieth high school reunion, many people remarked about my youthful appearance. That would not have occurred ten years ago. Conni and her staff are consummate professionals and, perhaps more importantly, caring individuals who make a *difference in the lives of their clients*.

This exercise will help return you to your natural posture; plus it feels good. Let yourself fall in love with the foam roller.

Step 3: The Foam Roller

Everyone should have one of these, and if you don't already, you can pick one up easily at an exercise supply center or Perform Better, an online exercise supply company. It is a long roller that looks like a pool noodle. Almost every gym or studio has one. You can select from harder ones to softer ones, depending on your comfort level.

The foam roller uses self-myofascial release techniques on the body. It releases the fascia, which is a sheet of fibrous connective tissue that envelops, separates, or binds together muscles, organs, and other soft structures of the body. Day-to-day working in front of the computer, driving, cooking, sewing, studying, texting, etc. can cause one to hold stress in the front shoulders, neck, and upper back. Lying on the foam roller will address most of the stresses from daily activities. Place the roller horizontally on the floor. Now, slowly go down to the floor. Your hips should be at one end and your head at the other. Make sure your back is completely on the roller. With head and hips supported, let your arms open out to the side and the backs of your hands drop down to touch the floor. Your knees should be bent with your feet on the floor, allowing the knees to roll in and touch one another. Make sure every part of your body is comfortable. If not, adjust to what's needed. If the roller is too hard, put a blanket on top of it for more comfort. That's it. Take deep breaths while you are here and enjoy. Don't rush. This is a perfect place to practice your focused breathing. Try lying here for five to ten minutes. Take about ten deep, full breaths. If we all took the time to do this one exercise, we would be in a better place in our bodies.

It feels good!

All you need to do is lie on the roller for the first time, and you'll understand what I mean. It is truly a delicious exercise. Inhale and take a deep breath in, and then exhale and relax. That's it! I want you to breathe and allow your upper body to open. It should feel good, with no pain anywhere. This is the most heart-opening exercise there is. Close your eyes, and with each breath, allow your spine to melt into the roller. I want you to feel very comfortable for this one.

After five to ten minutes of lying on the roller and breathing, the upper body starts to release. Now you can slowly move into arm circles on the roller. Before you start the arm circles, make sure you have full use of your shoulders. If there is any pain or restriction in the shoulders, keep your arms down by your side, palms facing up. There should be no pain anywhere. Slowly lift your arms up to the ceiling and then over your head into a slow and deliberate circle. Circle your arms slowly five times in one direction and slowly five times in the other. Feel as if you are moving through water. Slow and easy. Finish up with the arms out to the side for a final rest position.

After a few final breaths, slowly roll off the roller and lie on the floor just to see how open the spine feels. Do this exercise often. Leave your foam roller out where you can see it with a note on it that says: Use me.

Recap Chapter 3

The Fatal Error

1. When do you walk away from difficult events and people in your life? Is walking away easy or hard?
2. Dr. Brené Brown says joy comes to us in ordinary moments.
   Be grateful for what you have. Don't squander joy.
3. Amy Cuddy says change your posture for two minutes a day, and you can change your life. If you stand tall before meetings and new opportunities instead of crossing your arms and keeping yourself small, your life will change.
4. How do you stand tall? Stand in front of a mirror and stand as tall as you can, as if your head is a balloon rising up to the ceiling, neck relaxed, shoulders relaxed and, abdominals engaged, feet planted on the ground. Nothing in the body too tight or clenched. Easy and open. Close your eyes and breathe.
5. Use the foam roller. Lie down lengthwise, hips at one end and head on the other end of the roller, arms out to the side and relaxed on the floor with palms up, feet wide and knees dropped in and resting on one another. The foam roller allows the body to open and release at the same time, in an effortless way.

Chapter 4

The Excuse

What's your excuse? Why are you not doing it, being it, having it, living it, making it, seeing it, hearing it, feeling it, remembering it? What are you not doing that is keeping you so stuck?

What is keeping you in quicksand in your life? Every time you take a step forward, you slide back under. You keep letting it happen, and then you justify it. Why? What makes that so easy for you to keep doing? Does it feels normal for it to be that way? Perhaps you haven't listened to your own voice for so long that it seems weird to start now. No one wants to go out of their comfort zone and be uncomfortable. It doesn't feel right and doesn't feel good.

Neale Donald Walsch has a quote: "Life begins at the end of your comfort zone." I have that on my studio wall, and I look at it often to remind myself to get out of my way. There are days that the message slaps me in the face for my wake-up call.

There it is in a nutshell: not wanting to move out of our comfort zone, which keeps us from changing, keeps us from feeling the hurt, pain, disappointment, and making a sacrifice. Ah, there is that word: *sacrifice*. The definition of sacrifice is the act of giving up something that is valuable to you in order to help someone else. How do we translate that in our own lives? Do we walk away from food that isn't good for us? Maybe turn off the television at night and go out for a walk or read a book? Go to a class even though we don't want to because at the end of the class we know we will feel better. What can you do in your life that will make a change for the better? What sacrifice can bring you closer to your new goals? Embrace it and start taking the bold, new steps in your new direction and see what amazing miracles begin to happen.

I was at a small downtown Los Angeles screening of a movie made by an old friend of mine, and in walked one of the stars of the film, who was a little thicker around the middle. I began in that moment to judge everything about her in relationship to my body. Out of my mouth came, "Wow, she really hasn't taken of herself." In the next moment, my husband leaned over and said, "What, are you crazy? I'd tap that." And then I realized I had betrayed all of us—women, I mean. I had become a judger, a woman who looks at other women and comments on whatever doesn't look right about them, and I was sick! You know the type—one who whispers when another woman who might be younger or prettier walks into a room, a woman who comments on how another woman is wearing an outfit.

My job is to work with people on their body issues, except it seemed I had issues about my own body. I was getting thicker around the middle too. Yes, I work out and eat right, but I do drink wine, and wine converts to fat which goes right to the waist after a certain age. I hate when people single out a body part and become obsessed and crazy about it, but here I was doing just that. The reason is the widening of that body part is what I have been dealing with, as many women do as they move into their later fifties and sixties; it had become thick on me too. So instead of lovingly dealing with my stuff, I turned it on another woman.

Really, I was very upset, and I know how much we all deal with this every day: the whole mean girl thing and the messages we get from the media about how we should look at certain ages. In my early twenties I had a friend who was a model, and I witnessed the craziness that went down between all those beautiful women—my friend and her model friends who never felt good enough and were continually competing with one another. Just hanging out with them, wondering where that left me, was very intimating. I was eight inches shorter than they were. I felt that they had nothing to complain about. They had it all: beauty, height, money, fame, and yet that was not what was going on inside their brains. All they focused on was what they didn't have.

My husband, on the other hand, wasn't looking at that when the actress walked into the screening; he saw her overall beauty, which, by the way, she had in spades. He saw her sparkle and the beauty she had, and honestly, he didn't really care about her waist, just the way he didn't really care about that on me. It was me, all me, obsessing about an area and not looking at the bigger picture. I had been a feminist all my life, and here I was sinking to a new level and it was a low one. The minute I let go of my judgment I saw her light too, which was pretty amazing by the way, and she was great in the movie also. So how many other times has this happened in my life, where I have judged something so harshly that I took myself out of the connection with another person when it was my issue I was judging and the other person had very little to do with it?

The issue is not only connection with a person, but letting the ego hold onto a version of you that might not be realistic. Listen, I want to look as good as I can for as long as I can. I take care of my body and my skin, and I feel I look pretty good. But I am not twenty anymore. I have a beautiful nineteen-year-old daughter, and I love her skin and body and it makes me smile. Yeah, I remember that I used to have that great skin and small waist. I wouldn't trade my life now to be younger or have lots more collagen in my skin. (Well, maybe just a little.) I appreciate my body giving me two beautiful children and so many crazy life experiences. So maybe it's not as tight as it used to be, but the trade-off was worth it. When I turned fifty, all the media talked about was how fifty was the new thirty, but moving forward and turning sixty, I must deal with getting older. Aging is inevitable, and I am wiser. I talk with my daughter and her friends, doling out small bits of wisdom when I think they will listen. I love having new teachers in my studio, watching them grow and learn and mentoring them.

As we enter new decades, I think we must redefine ourselves. I think we must mentor younger men and women. Go inward and think about how we want to feel and allow ourselves to change. Aging is not the enemy. Isn't the enemy how we think about aging, the stories we tell ourselves, and the stories the media tells us and we believe? The airbrushing, the lies they tell us to keep us feeling bad so we buy whatever product? I work with some amazing men and women in their seventies and eighties, and they are all such an inspiration to me— energetic, full of life, involved in the world and with other people, traveling, loving life, doing Pilates, and keeping their bodies active. That's who I want to be. As we get older, there is a loss of what we had with the younger us, and yet, we are growing to a different, and hopefully better, place.

I'm going to make this personal. It wasn't easy to write this. What I mean is I got halfway through, and it wasn't easy to finish. I would do anything other than write. All of a sudden I needed to clean the house or run an errand or watch all the shows I'd recorded—anything and everything but write. Does that seem familiar to any of you?

Not only that, but I left the Pilates studio I had been in for thirteen years. I was tired of losing money and going further into debt over something that I loved. The model for the business was not working, and honestly, I was killing myself and neglecting my family. Everything was being drained from me, especially my bank account. I had to stop the bleeding, so I pulled the plug on the way the business was being run. I closed the big 2,000-square-foot studio and moved into a sweet 500 square feet of calm. It took me a long time to get there. The thought of all of it was so overwhelming and scary. I kept dreaming of another way to run the business, and all I could think about was selling it, but that didn't work out.

Funny how providence has a way of showing up in your life and leading you down the right road, literally driving the right road. I saw a sign, drove past it a couple of times, and saw my new place. How was I going to get there? How was I going to make it work out? One day something in me snapped, and I'd had it with my landlords. I was tired of them not treating me well, raising the rent while having me do all the work, and never taking care of anything. I was done! I got in my car and went down a different street, and there it was. I kept going past it, and then I called. Things end up showing up just when you need them if you open your eyes. I said yes to the new space, and things fell into place rapidly. It was the deciding that took me so long. It was the fear of the what-if. What if no one liked it or I lost all my clients? None of that mattered because I was so disconnected, and that kept me stuck in myself and totally out of joy for a long time. It also kept the people I cared about out of joy too—my kids and my husband. I didn't realize they were getting my leftovers, my emotional leftovers, and that was not good.

I knew I really wanted to finish my book and knew I had something to say, but I let things continue to stop me. Stopping me from having joy were the same feelings that had been stopping me all my life from getting what I need and want. It wasn't outside of me, but inside, it was *me*. I was the problem. No other excuse but me: I was the one holding myself back.

Holding back from the person you care about the most sounds crazy, but it happens. Why would we do that to ourselves? Now that you know your personal demon, you can begin to deal with it. You can begin to self-heal, or, rather, self-deal. Begin the process of self-dealing and learning how to care for you. Put yourself back in the center of your life, front and center, not in the back row where so many of us live and feel comfortable. Right there is the first row, center seat. Maybe even be kind to yourself; treat yourself like you would a friend— someone you really care about who is having a hard time and maybe needs a little extra TLC. Ha-ha, isn't that the crazy part? We aren't really nice to ourselves at all.

I've made a decision to change that. I am going to become best friends with me. Yep, that's right, my new BFF: I've started to take myself to lunch, spend time alone, and ask myself how I am feeling, and I'm going to start to listen. I will become nicer to myself; I always make all my clients work on their self-care, so I think it's time to take my own advice. I going to enjoy getting a massage, spending time in nature, working out, and reading all the things that I love. Not just work. Give myself the space to really explore what I like and what gives me joy.

The client for this one is me.

Every day I give myself thirty minutes of me time. It doesn't matter what time it is, but it's time just for me. When my daughter was born and my son was having a hard time adjusting, I was working with the director of our preschool and she gave me the suggestion of spending thirty minutes a day of special time with him, doing whatever he wanted to do. This allowed him to run the show, so to speak, and gave him total focus time. The only restriction was we couldn't go in the car for a big drive; it would have to something at home or a walk. Once the thirty minutes was over, we stopped and continued on the next day. And this, I realized, is what we need for ourselves—a look at what we need in our daily lives: time in meditation, lunch with a friend, a walk in the park, sitting outside with a cup of tea, a class we've wanted to take, or hanging out on the foam roller. Thirty minutes of special time for yourself can be difficult to find, but you are well worth it; give yourself that gift. All of it is valid, whether it be painting, dancing, gardening, or merely listening to your inner voice. That voice has always been there; we just don't make time to listen. Your inner voice is one the most important voices to listen to.

For my birthday two years ago I went off and experienced two weekends of yoga nidra, which is a sleep guided meditation. Going inward. My friend John Vosler teaches yoga nidra and has a website where you can get cd's and mp3s: https://johnvosler.com. John is fantastic; he pushes you inward. John is a senior teacher of the yoga nidra professional training at the Amrit Yoga Institute. He has had a long history in psycho-structural balancing and is a Pilates teacher, bodyworker, yoga teacher, and yoga nidra teacher. He is well-rounded in all of his experiences and grounded in *joy*.

I asked John my joy questions, which you must make sure you answer for yourself.

Question: If you were to define joy, what would it be?

John: "A feeling of peace and love in action."

Q: What happens when you are aware that joy is missing?

John: "I recognize that I am ignoring my true nature. When I see that joy is missing, I also see how tired I am and how much I am doing for others without caring for myself. In those moments, I start to breathe life back into my being, and I remind myself of the eternal truth that I am."

Q: What is a pivotal moment that you have had with joy?

John: "It came in a meditation, and I felt that feeling of being separate and of being whole at the same time. I felt complete."

Q: What takes you out of joy?

John: "The feeling of doing and thinking too much takes me out of joy, not being balanced in my life."

Q: Do you have any routines that put you back into joy?

John: "What puts me back into my joy zone is yoga nidra, meditation, dance, tennis, love, living in each moment with pure abandonment."

My exercise is a love letter to yourself, letting you know what you did right in your life.

Step 4: A Loving Letter to Your Younger Self from Your Future Self

I started to think about this when my son and daughter had to go off on a retreat for school. The parents had to write letters to their children, telling them what they had done right in their lives, and it got me thinking. When do we do that for ourselves? We will drop everything to do it for others, but we will not make the effort to ascertain what we really need to hear from our own deepest self.

Write a letter of love and support to yourself, letting yourself know how the mistakes that you made were perfect for you and led you to your greatest successes. We learn more from our mistakes than from anything else. It is easy to live in the successes, but our mistakes make us grow and make different choices.

Let your younger self know that you send love and support as you would to a dear friend. Here is my letter to my younger self:

My dearest Conni,

This letter has been a long time coming. I'm sorry for its delay, and I didn't realize how much you needed a letter. I want you to know how much I deeply love you and how wonderful I think you are; how beautiful, kind, and smart; and how loving you are of others. I know you doubt yourself often, but I am here to tell you there has been no need. Most of the steps you took that were uncertain turned out to be your best ones. I know you have been worried about your future and if things would turn out for you, and they have—in more beautiful ways than you ever thought possible. When you were younger, your dream was to be a dancer, and then after you stopped dancing, an actress was what you thought you needed to be. But you took all those wonderful qualities and rolled them up into a new career: your love of teaching movement with your love of working with people. You have made your life's work the place where you shine, teaching Pilates and making people love to move and feel good in their bodies. You are a success because you love what you do, and your life has flourished.

You met the man of your dreams and the love of your life and have been married twenty-five years. I know it sounds like a long time, but it is a flash—a flash of good times and difficult times all rolled up into a wonderful relationship. You have two beautiful and funny kids, Joey and Hannah, and they astound you and keep you on your toes. Your family is the joy of your life, and I know you waited a long time to have them. You have beaten yourself up in the past for what you thought was important or what you thought you needed to do, but I am here to tell you it wasn't important. You are a good mother, friend, wife, woman, teacher, and boss. You are a force to be reckoned with. I am so proud of you for all that you have accomplished. Don't worry and don't stress; it never helps you, and most of the time it stops you in your tracks and keeps you from moving forward. Trust in yourself and know deep in your heart that things will work out. They will work out better than you have even imagined. I need you to start thinking bigger and better, and the universe will give you even more.

People are longing to hear what you have to say and what your spin is on it. Don't censor yourself; forget about being scared; do it anyway. You won't be able to stop the fear, so keep moving through it. Speak your truth; at the end of the day, that is all you have. Believe it and stay focused. Let yourself be alive, and live in the moment as much as you can. Know that I am always in your corner, pushing you forward. I have always believed in you no matter what. Stay true to your inner voice; it will never lead you down the wrong path.

All my love,

Future Conni

Recap Chapter 4

The Excuse

1. What's your excuse for not having the life you want?
2. Neale Donald Walsch: "Life begins at the end of your comfort zone."
3. Give yourself thirty minutes of me time—time that you can use to do anything you want. Here are some suggestions: read, bathe, workout, and run, have a cup of tea, paint, color, or walk in nature. Do something that makes your heart sing.
4. John Vosler and yoga nidra sleep guided meditation.
5. Loving letter to your younger self from your future self.

Chapter 5

Centered within Self— Not Self-Centered

When we feel better, we deal better.

A better connection to ourselves and connection to spirit—that's what we are all looking for. Have you ever been in a place where everything clicks? Where everything feels like it is flowing together? You get every green light, the day feels seamless, all your interactions are fulfilling, all your commitments are honored for the day, and you are truly living in the zone. That feeling is being in the flow and trusting that all is well in your life, you will be taken care of, and everything will work out as it should. How can we have more of those days? Is it our perception of the day and focusing on the positive outcome? Why do some days flow so perfectly? What does living in the flow even mean, and how do we stay there? Can we allow ourselves to have good feelings and keep them? Can we allow ourselves to live in that higher vibrational space and trust that when we fall off course, and we will, that we know we can jump or crawl right back to that higher vibrational feeling?

I wrote about this earlier. We are so worried about people calling us self-centered that we don't listen to our inner callings. What if we reframe the way we talk about the self and keep ourselves centered within?

Centered within Self, Not Self-Centered.

One of my clients said that to me one day, and it was like a bell went off in my head. I said, "That's it!" That's the way we need to think of it. I love that. Thank you, Sharon G.

It begins with changing the concept of who we think we are. In his book, *Wishes Fulfilled: Mastering the Art of Manifesting*, Dr. Wayne Dyer talks about changing from an ordinary life to an extraordinary life:

> I'm inviting you to be receptive to a radical new idea about yourself. It's radical because ever since you left your mother's womb, you've been subjected to cultural conditioning designed to help you be content with living a "normal life" at the level of ordinary consciousness, which generally means accepting whatever life hands you. In many ways you've been programmed to believe that you do not have the wisdom or ability to manifest the fulfillment of your wishes or desires.

I am saying as clearly as I [can]: *There's a plane of awareness that you can opt to live at, wherein you can, if you are willing to change your concept of yourself as an ordinary being, find yourself fulfilling any and all wishes you have for yourself.*

...I would like to offer a few words on...two concepts of ordinary and extraordinary.

Ordinary is, well so ordinary. It means that you do all the things that your culture and family have programmed you to do. It implies that you fit in, study hard, follow the rules, take care of your obligations, fill out the forms, pay your taxes, get a job...and then you retire, play with your grandchildren, and ultimately die. I want to emphasize there is nothing wrong with this scenario...

Extraordinary encompasses most of the ordinary, since we all live in the same physical world. There will be forms to fill out, rules that demand our obedience, bills to pay, and family obligations to attend to. But extraordinary consciousness is associated with your soul, that invisible, boundaryless energy that looks out from behind your eyeballs and has very different interests than the ordinary self does.

> The idea of your soul, the thing that it yearns for, is not more knowledge.
>
> ...Your invisible self is extraordinary because it is a fragment of the universal soul, which is infinite. The part of you that knows that you have greatness, and is stirred by the idea of you expanding and removing any and all limitations, is what I am addressing...This is your new self-concept, one inspired by your soul. (Dyer, 2012, pp.26–27)

I love Dr. Wayne Dyer and have read his books for years. When he died in August 2015, I was compelled to read and reread all of his works. I felt as if he were speaking to me, and I should be listening. I did start listening and living more in the moment, following what I know is my purpose.

In this next section I want to try to uncover a few ways we can go off course. And ways that we can start to notice how we go off course.

There are always people out there who will steal your joy. They are usually so sneaky about it we don't even notice at first. I call these people or the situations killjoys. We all have them; they are holes in our lives that can actually drain our joy. We walk away from these situations and feel bad— bad about ourselves or what just happened—and we are usually not sure why. There are people who can drain our joy, and there are situations that can drain our joy.

We don't always realize that we allow people or situations to drain us until we feel that somewhat yucky feeling every time we are around or after we leave certain people. That creepy, in-the-pit-of-your-stomach feeling—it tends to sneak up on us and only later do we feel it. We keep thinking it must be us; those people are friends, right?

Finding where we are allowing killjoys into our lives can take a little digging. They are usually very sneaky in their carving out a piece of us.

Let's take some time and explore this. If you had to pick one killjoy in your life, what would it be? Think about it. Is it a person, a situation, or a place that makes you feel less than the best that you can feel? If every time you are with that person or in that situation or place you feel bad about yourself when you leave, why are you so stuck staying there? What would it take for you to move out of that environment? Why do you allow someone else to make decisions about your life?

Here are some major killjoys to get you thinking:

Fear killjoy: the inability to take the first step, being afraid to make a change in case it is the wrong move or wrong decision; it feels like everything is stopping us in our tracks. Procrastination is a big part of fear. Fear keeps us down and tethered to lots of insecurities.

Depression killjoy: feeling hopeless, lethargic, stuck, lost, and unable to move in any way. In depression we stop all movement, because that keeps us down and feeling bad—right where depression wants us. As we start to move more in our bodies, depression starts to have less of a hold on our outlook. If we continue moving even when we don't want to, we begin to move into having better feelings slowly over time. Movement moves us through depression into better-feeling places.

Isolation killjoy: feeling and being separate from others, alone, afraid, nowhere to turn. In isolation, we sink deeper and deeper inward and lose our connection with the outside world. Our world becomes much smaller. There is a feeling of no hope, no way out.

Stress killjoy: allowing others to take over our time, being overworked and overextended. Maybe we are making a life transition; maybe we are unable to say no, unable to make good choices for ourselves, and have poor self-care. The stressed person is so overloaded in their nerve endings that they overreact to most situations.

Are any of these or a combination of these killjoys holding you back in your life? Remember there are only two emotions we function out of: fear or love.

Which of these is in your life?

Tanna's story:

Tanna Marshall Benedict is a life coach, a writer, a holistic health practitioner, and a wonderful human being. She was laid off from Capitol Records, where she had worked for twenty years, and her father had asked her to live with her mom because he was dying. She moved in with her mom because she was starting to decline into Alzheimer's, and Tanna took over managing her health. She found a day care facility for both seniors and children. Her mom had been a preschool teacher for thirty-three years, so the little ones were extra special to her.

Tanna used her knowledge of holistic health and started changing her mother's daily routines. Her health has improved, and her decline has slowed. Tanna changed her mom's diet to a gluten-free one, and she lost thirty pounds. Her mom's blood pressure is now normal, and her cholesterol is perfect. She has been doing physical therapy and has a daily exercise routine that keeps her body strong, and she works on her balance, and she encourages her mom to be more self-sufficient, as much as she possibly can. They have a great time together, and she makes sure there is lots of laughter and fun, especially regarding her situation, to help keep the energy light and joyful. She even tells her mom secrets and lets her know she is doing so because she knows she wouldn't remember. Her mom loves that.

I asked Tanna my questions about joy.

Question: What is joy to you?

Tanna: "To me, joy is a warm glow from within that radiates out to everyone around me."

Q: What happens when you are aware that joy is missing?

Tanna: "When I notice that I am not feeling good, I bring myself back to the elements of my life that I appreciate and make me feel good and joyful. The joy is there; I just get distracted and need to remind myself to focus."

Q: Have you had a pivotal moment with joy?

Tanna: "My most pivotal moment came last year when my book *The Enlightened Caregiver* came out. I realized that for over five years I had battled with myself over where to focus my attention. Build a life coaching business, take care of my mom. I was constantly divided, always in a state of conflict.

"I felt frustrated with the stagnation of the business and resentful of taking care of my mom. I could never fully focus on both, so I let go of the struggle with my business and made caring for my mother my number-one priority. I had to admit that I was a full-time caregiver. Now I am able to give more love, attention, and better care to my mother. I feel better about myself and my role as caretaker. Taking the pressure off myself has made my life much more enjoyable, and I know I will look back at this time with my mom as incredibly precious."

Q: What takes you out of joy?

Tanna: "The thing that takes me out of joy the fastest is comparing myself to others and being self-critical. I limit my time on Facebook and watching TV. It's too easy to look at others and think, 'Wow they are doing so well and I am not.' Comparison kills self-love and self-esteem."

Q: Do you have any daily routines that keep you in joy?

Tanna: "Meditation, exercise, spending time in nature every day, continually bringing my attention back to myself and my personal bubble of joy and positivity. I also visit the happiest place on earth, *Disneyland*, a lot. That puts me right into joy."

Step 5: The Restorative Power of Water and Bodywork

I want to talk about baths and the restorative power of water. Most of us do not know how to relax. It is not something that is supported by our culture. So, we have to put our bodies in an environment that supports us. Taking a bath with Epsom salts and relaxing for twenty minutes takes a layer of stress out of your life. It is a glass of wine for your body. Set yourself up for relaxation. Dim the lights. Light a candle. Set in place a neck pillow so you can relax, or roll up a towel and put it behind your head. Put on soft music, or just let your mind wander. Put three to four cups of Epsom salts in the bathwater and just let yourself soak. Clear your head, breathe, and let yourself go. Remember the old commercial slogan "Calgon take me away?" That is exactly what you want to let yourself do—be taken away for a few minutes from all the stress, worry, and challenges of your day. Breathe and just let yourself go and unwind. Breathing and bathing both take toxins out of the body. Bodywork is another fantastic choice whether it is massage, acupuncture, craniosacral work, or seeing a chiropractor, paying attention and listening to the body are key.

Letting someone else take care of you is total self-care. Letting a professional help you when you are out of alignment and not feeling good or alive in your body can allow you to heal faster. Take your hands off the wheel, so to speak, and allow your body to rest and rejuvenate.

Recap Chapter 5

Centered within Self—Not Self-Centered

1. When we feel better, we deal better.
2. Change the concept of who we think we are. Check out Dr. Wayne Dyer "Wishes Fulfilled: Mastering the Art of Manifesting."
3. Plan to go from an ordinary life to an extraordinary life.
4. Where and who are the kill joys in your life? Find those holes and fill them up.
5. Enjoy the restorative power of water and bodywork.

Chapter 6

The Vision

The greatest gift we can give is to allow ourselves to open up to a new vision of how we want our lives to look.

What would it look like if you landed in the middle of your wildest dreams? Who would you be? How big or crazy can you imagine? Can you even imagine that?

After I had my children, I was loving being a mom but really floundering in my sense of self. I didn't know where to look. I read books and talked with other moms and discovered that many of us felt the same. I wanted to work and was moving between a few ideas, but nothing struck home. I was lost, depressed, unjoyful, and wasn't moving very much, except for running after kids. I was fat, and I found it hard to make time to exercise. I had stopped caring about myself and how I looked. Everything else in my life went to the top, and I put myself last on my list.

I hate to admit that, but it was true. All my focus had gone into my children, my husband, and my home. There was not much left over for me. One day I caught my reflection, and I knew I needed to change. You know the vision: mom jeans, poor posture, hurried, fat, and not feeling in my body at all. I started walking every day, and I started to feel better; the more I moved, the better I felt and looked. I knew that I was on the right track. I knew that it had to be with movement that I needed to focus, and that's when I started teaching prenatal and postnatal exercise classes. I was a mom, and many friends had small children, so I recruited most of our nursery school into classes, and that felt really good. I was keeping it close to my interests and I knew I was on the right path.

Sometimes when we go off on our quest for our deepest desires, we look outside of ourselves, maybe missing something that is right within reach.

There are questions you need to ask yourself: What are your interests? What are your goals? Have you ever worked? What part of work did you like? Do you like people? What did you love to do as a child? Do you like to shop and help others? Are you volunteering anywhere? I always find if you have the time and are not sure what to do, there are so many places that need your help and could use your enthusiasm and hard work, and finding those places might land you right in the middle of your wildest dreams.

All right, so you are there in the middle of your wildest dreams. How does it look? Now what? What do you want to happen? How do you want to feel? How do you want to look? Where do you live? What are you wearing? How do you sound? What's on your walls? What kind of music do you like? We can go on and on like this, but the answers are very important. They will shape what happens to you in your life and now plan out how you want your future to look. Don't sweat the how! Just get into the feeling of what you want your life to look like and keep dreaming on that.

My wildest dream became being a transformational movement teacher and lifestyle coach and changing people's lives, owning a Pilates studio, working and traveling the world with Crystal Cruise Lines, writing and reading this book, and envisioning a radio show. Who knows where else joy will take me! Think big—beyond what you can believe—and then think even bigger and see what the universe has in store for you. We keep ourselves kind of small, but if we can go beyond the defined, as my friend and mentor Marsh Engle says, we can open up to a new definition of ourselves. We are always looking to redefine the next chapter of our lives and how we want that to feel. We want to move from our feeling selves, not from what we think others want us to do or what we should do.

So we need a definition that makes us expand. Now, what if the divide between us, our dreams, and how we think of ourselves is too wide? To change that we must not change our dreams, but expand how we define and look at ourselves.

Anne's story:

My friend Anne has always lived a bigger-than-life life. She has been an actress for more than thirty years, working in the soaps, theater, and television. We have stayed close for all of these years. We met in acting class thirty years ago and bonded over bad acting scenes, with me mostly acting badly in class. I would throw fake grenades at bad scenes and we would laugh and try to be quiet, and I guess that bonded us for life. Time carried us through boyfriends, husbands, different cities, and children. Her dream of being an actor has never wavered. She has always done the work and pushed when the rest of us got tired and couldn't do it anymore. She kept sending out résumés; meeting directors and agents; doing plays and film; and whatever needed to be done. That's why she keeps working as an actor. She keeps changing the definition of herself and expanding it to include new avenues of experiences to make her résumé better and expand her horizons.

Over time, even living in the same city we would only see each other two to three times a year: busy lives, careers, and children. That changed in 2012. She was in a motorcycle accident that year. A car cut her off, she fell, and her motorcycle fell on her, almost crushing her foot. The good news is she escaped with only a bad foot injury, instead of something worse. As soon as I heard the news, I went over to her house. I was happy that she was okay, but I knew she had a long road ahead of her. She was lucky to have only hurt her foot, but it was still very traumatic. I was glad to be there and to be able to help her move and talk and just be with her. I know I had forgotten how wonderful female friendships are, especially the ones that have stood the test of time. I had to ask Anne my joy questions, and here is what she said;

Question: If you were to define joy, what would it be?

Anne: "Joy is an open heart at play; it feels free and expansive. It has no boundaries or limitations. Joy is abundant and available whenever we're ready to receive it."

Q: What happens when you are aware that joy is missing in your life?

Anne: "When joy is missing, I feel dull and lifeless; I am secluded, boarded up, closed in. I get quiet and introspective, and I hibernate and alienate myself from others. When I am not in joy, I get jealous and wish I could be someone else, somewhere else, and I wish my life was other than what it is."

Q: How do you identify the missing pieces of joy and bring them in?

Anne: "I know that I am not in joy when I find myself in confusion, despair, or when I am feeling particularly lonely."

"That's when I know I've fallen out of joy. I get back by expressing gratitude for every single thing in my life. I make a list and am thankful for each and everything and that leads me to joy. Along with making a list of things I am grateful for, I also begin doing things I love again, like taking a bubble bath with candles and soft music, riding my bike, going on a long walk or a run, writing, painting, reading something inspirational, sharing meals with friends, and enjoying meaningful conversation."

Q: Did you have a pivotal moment with joy?

Anne: "I have experienced many moments of being in and out of joy over the years. When I feel sorry for myself and I wish things were other than what they are, it is a sure sign that I am no longer living in joy. Accidents are a big jolt out of joy.

"A pivotal moment when I felt out of joy was when I was in a motorcycle accident a few years ago. I was hit by an SUV while riding home after meeting my brother for lunch. I didn't see it coming and ended up in the ER with a crush injury. My left foot required seventeen stitches on one side and a surgery to pin the fifth metatarsal back on the other side."

Anne said she had enjoyed riding motorcycles safely for more than twelve years, so it was devastating to be involved in an accident. She said, "There's a saying in the motorcycle community: keep the rubber side down, and it's not if you go, it's when you go. But I never thought it would happen to me. I was a good and safe rider. My smile was never as big as when I was riding, and my riding buddies would tease me but I didn't care. Nothing made me happier.

"After the accident, I was definitely not happy or smiling. I was unable to ride but also unable to walk for six months, hopping along in a surgical boot, assisted with the aid of crutches, wondering if I would be able to walk normally again. I'm an actress, so I wasn't able to work except for voice-overs. Since acting brings me the greatest joy of all, not being able to work was particularly upsetting.

"That's when Conni and I reconnected. When I told her I was in an accident, she went into action, making the long drive over to my house every Thursday for three months. During that time she helped me get my body moving again, taking me through various exercises each week, always adding something new and challenging. It gave me so much encouragement to keep going and improving and watching my foot slowly improve over time. One day she brought a Hula-Hoop, and I panicked and said I can't do that! But she knew I could. It was fun and I found myself smiling for the first time in months. It felt so freeing to be able to hula-hoop.

"I had so many difficult moments as I found myself getting back to walking again, often breaking down into tears of frustration when I was unable to do certain things, like point my toe or do a calf raise, or, as it is called in ballet, a relevé on the ball of my foot. Since I had been a dancer, this was especially upsetting. But Conni was there for the constant reassurance that I would be able to do these things again in time. Exercise was crucial for a full recovery and I was willing to work hard.

"I had a lot of help during this challenging time. My family was there for me. My mom came over daily to cook meals, and my dad took me to the pool twice a week where I would walk around the shallow end. Unable to bear weight on land, I was allowed to move more freely in the water, without the use of crutches, and walking across the pool gave me the assurance that I would eventually walk on land soon.

"Although I was working hard and improving each day, I burst into tears with my physical therapist, Blake, one day. He handed me a box of tissues and asked if I was okay. 'I'm fine,' I sniffled, 'just feeling sorry for myself.' I was going to PT three times a week hoping for a speedy recovery only to learn the healing process was much slower than I had expected it to be and it was wearing thin on my patience. That's when I realized how far out of joy I had fallen. It was time to focus on the positive and envision the outcome I truly wanted, which was a healthy foot able to do all the things I loved to do.

"When I could drive again, I would make the weekly visit to Conni's studio and continued working with her. With her help and a lot of effort on my part, my foot found its way back to normal and its own joy.

"The accident could have been much worse and I found myself grateful for Conni's support and encouragement that my foot would not only be better, but that, in time, it would be better than ever. And it is!

"I continue to practice what makes me feel good and keeps me uplifted and joyful.

"Sometimes we need help finding our way back to joy. I am extraordinarily grateful that my family, friends, doctors, and therapists reached out to guide me and my foot back to joy again. It was an important journey that changed my life in a big way.

"During the healing process I allowed myself to live fully, saying yes to an oversea adventure with Conni aboard the Crystal Cruise Lines; then I sold my house in LA and moved back to NYC, where I am working as an actress and living my dream. It was a long road looking back. I see how every part of the journey was necessary and changed my life for the better. One thing I know to be true is that something positive always comes out of something that seems negative."

Q: What takes you out of joy?

Anne: "Worry. That takes me out of joy; negative comments or harsh critique delivered without kindness can quickly take me out of joy if I am not careful. My imagination is so active, so I have to be extremely cautious of giving my mind free rein, because it can spiral down and latch onto worry."

Q: Do you have a practice that keeps you in joy?

Anne: "Gratitude is essential for me, and I express all that I am grateful for on a daily basis. I keep a daily journal and am truly thankful for all that I have, trusting that I am exactly where I need to be. I don't wish for a different life."

One more quick story about Anne, I was offered a trip teaching Pilates with Crystal Cruises, and my husband lovingly stayed home with our daughter. He suggested taking Anne instead. She was almost healed, and it gave her an even greater incentive to get better. We traveled the world in an amazing way, met fantastic people, and had the time of our lives. We went on two cruises that year. Even though I would not wish an injury on anyone, what came out of Anne's injury was so amazing for both of us. You just never know what is around the corner.

We want to keep the joyous feelings in the forefront of our minds; we need to be aware of when we are feeling joy and when we are not.

Step 6: Joy Journal

This is how we start to notice that there might be joy hiding, and we don't even know it is there because we don't value it.

First, buy the journal that accompanies this book. It is a beautiful book you will want to write in. Write down your joys—little ones, big ones, any you can think of. Start small, noticing the little things around you everywhere: clouds in the sky, flowers in the spring, air on your skin, unexpected money in the mail, a call from an old friend.

Don't sensor yourself. Just notice. Write down everything and how it makes you feel. We want to cultivate more joy. Whatever we put our attention on expands. When we pay attention, miraculous things begin to happen.

Now list what would put you into more joy. How would you need to change or what would you need to do to have more joy in your life? Start to look at everything in a joyous way. The more you think about it, the more you will see it.

What keeps us in joy are our feelings of gratitude. So if you are struggling with finding joy, start by being and feeling grateful, and you will notice that the joy follows.

Write it down. When you write it down, you commit and it can happen because it is acknowledged in your mind. It becomes something to value. If you keep your journal close and just jot down what comes to mind, the process will begin to be more conscious over time. Keep it short if you're not sure what to say. Make your wildest dreams come true!

Recap Chapter 6

The Vision

1. The greatest gift we can give is to allow ourselves to be open to a new vision of how we want our life to be.
2. What would your life look like if you landed in the middle of your wildest dreams?
3. Ask yourself the joy questions.
4. If you were to define joy what would it be?
5. What happens when you are aware that joy is missing?
6. Have you had a pivotal moment with joy?
7. What takes you out of joy?
8. Do you have any routines that put you back into joy?
9. Joy journal: Write down your joy insights every day. The little ordinary ones that become extraordinary. The more you notice the joy all around you the more joy that will appear. Joy turns into gratitude.

Chapter 7

The Gateway

Passion is the new sexy.

How is the body a vessel for joy? Most of what we experience is in our physical bodies. We deal with the world through our feelings. We feel thirsty, we feel hungry, feel sexy, feel sleepy, feel nervous, feel joy, anger, hate, love, and on and on. We are feeling beings, and yet, most of us get so mucked up because we put our head into it (a.k.a. our egos), and then off we spin into crazy time. We have lost our connection with our feelings, and that translates to losing our connection to ourselves, which can translate into stress, depression, and getting upset; we get taken out of our lives yet again. We feel the air on our skin, love in our hearts, and loss in our gut, and the more attuned we become to listening to our bodies, the faster we can deal with issues that come up. And issues will always come up; that's what makes us human. Do we deal with them or try to push them under the rug? Our bodies are always talking to us, but are we listening? Really listening such that if we are in pain, do we feel it? Do we know what hunger feels like? We know when our bodies are sick and unhealthy most times, but on the other side, do we know when our bodies are alive and robust, feeling unbounded joy? Do we know that feeling?

Everything in the universe is made of up of energy. We can't see it, but it is there. Albert Einstein said nothing happens until something moves. It is the chain of events that gets everything going and the ball rolling. The vibration of joy is very high. When we are vibrating at a higher level, everything seems to go smoother in our lives, and we seem to feel better in our bodies. We know the feeling: everything goes right for us in the day; we hit every green light; the phone rings and it is someone we haven't spoken to in a long time; all of our interactions in the day are good ones; and there is a bounce in our steps.

I started asking around about joy to see what people would say, and most of the answers were very similar. Lori Shayew was kind enough to answer some questions about joy. For more than twenty years her work has centered on autism and changing people's perception of it. Her company is called The Gifts of Autism, and she works not only with the children, but focuses on the parents as well. Her position is that children are fully functioning on a higher vibrational level and are whole and perfect. It is the parents and society at large who have the problem. All they see is the deficit—the children not fitting in or functioning as they would have them function. Lori helps parents raise their *joy* vibration so they can get in sync with their children's natural joy.

Lori says, "I've worked directly with autistic kids for over twenty years now, and from my perspective, these kids are wired for joy. It is their natural state. They do not water down this emotion for anyone. They have no filter and do not worry about what others think about them; they don't care. I call it unbounded *joy*. I cannot be in a room with a child in *full-out joy* and not want to join them in a joy-filled state. Many times my cheeks start hurting from smiling so big and long."

I asked Lori my joy questions.

Question: If you were to define joy, what would it be?

Lori: "Unbounded freedom, a very high vibration. No holding back. Pure bliss. The vibration of *joy* = magic."

Q: What happens when joy is missing?

Lori: "Things don't flow as grooveliciously. It is a sign that we are out of alignment with the natural state of being."

Q: How do you identify the missing pieces of joy and bring them in?

Lori: "When things don't flow for me, something is missing. Usually there is some self-doubt, judgment, fears occurring somewhere in my body. To get myself back to *joy*, I must release judgment (self-forgiveness is one way), and then I find uplifting activities: people, good conversations can lift my vibration. Sometimes all it takes is petting my cat to lift my joy vibe. It's good to be aware of how I lift myself. Also, music is a big lifter for me, as well as the beach. Worry, self-doubt, and fear all take me out of joy."

Q: Have you had a pivotal moment with joy?

Lori: "A few months ago, I was returning from a retreat and decided to go for a walk. I was filled with gratitude and joy, not a negative thought in my head. I started noticing things during my walk that I hadn't noticed before. At one point, I passed a passion fruit tree and noticed an abundance of passion fruit. I asked myself why I haven't seen this tree before. I heard this voice inside of me say, because your vibration wasn't high enough! I continued walking and noticed a front yard filled with various animals: peacocks, squirrels, birds, cats, etc. I felt like I was watching a cartoon, like *Bambi*, where everyone was coexisting. That was my sign, which told me I was in the vibration of *joy*. It was pure magic."

Q: Think into your life. Have you ever had an experience of pure joy? What was it? What made it different from the other special moments in your life?

Lori: "Interviewing people on my podcast. Giving a voice to the gift beyond the label gives me so much joy. At first I was overwhelmed by the process, but after some practice and self-confidence, I found that the interview process energized me. Joy comes at the completion of the podcast. It is a feeling of bliss. I think the reason is I am talking about something that I am passionate about, and my guest is always in alignment with me. It is so much fun!"

What are you passionate about? Can you dig deep and find that answer, or does it totally elude you?

I feel talking about passion leads us into sensuality. What is sensuality? It is the enjoyment of pleasure that we get from our five senses: sight, hearing, taste, smell, and touch. Sensual is more about actions and behavior— how you walk, eat, taste, smell, and touch.

Then what is sexy? Are they different?

Sexy is generally more about looks directly—what you wear, the shape of your body, hair style, that kind of thing. You could dress conservatively and still be sensual. "Sensual is better than sexy," says Yahoo! answers. "Most girls can't pull off sensual without getting sexy in some part of it."

Sensuality means fulfilling to the senses. Have you ever thought or do you even think about your senses or how they feel and what that means to you in this moment?

If we are living from joy and including it in our lives and valuing the information that it brings us, then we need to include sensual living too. How can we do that? It is important to notice how we feel in our bodies and in our skin. As we get older, sometimes we seem to cut that part of ourselves off. We forget our physical selves. We don't think about sensuality or sexuality as much. Can we move through the world in a more sensual way as we age? Also, can we use our senses in a more conscious way? Can we think about sensuality even if we don't have a partner?

I believe we can, because it has nothing to do with anyone else. It is about ourselves and how we move in the world, the way our eyes see and negotiate the world around us, and the way we take things in. The way we allow our bodies to feel as we move throughout our days.

We can't talk about sensuality without everyone jumping on the sexy bandwagon. I love sexy. To me, it is feeling very alive in my body, but I'm talking about something very different. Honestly, they both get a bad rap. Talk about being around someone sexy or really living in a sensual way, and you hear all kinds of comments. I hear such comments mostly from other women. Marianne Williamson the author of *Return to Love: Reflections on the Principles of a Course of Miracles*. 'says we come from one of two places: fear or love. You tell me: Which feeling are you living from? Women don't like it, and most men do. Why do jealous or mean thoughts come from other women? How come we don't support each other? Where does the jealousy come from? Misunderstanding? Self-loathing? Envy?

I would see it with my daughter in school—the whole mean girl thing. The girls would pick one girl and start to exclude her from activities, and they would all join in, hurting and, I feel, breaking the spirit of the girl who had been made the outcast. As far as I know, boys do not do this. As women, we grow up, but this behavior still seems to persist.

So what is it that I am talking about? What does sensuality have to teach us? I think sensuality teaches us about self-love.

Here are some questions I want you to think about and write about. Take time thinking about each one. Allow the answers to come to you. If they don't come at first, let the questions sit and ponder what your ideas might be. Nothing is written in stone, so allow yourself to daydream.

- Are you at the center of your life?
- Do you value your voice and your time?
- Are you following your heart's desire?
- Are you taking care of your own needs?
- Are you taking responsibility for your life and happiness?
- Are you treating yourself with love and kindness?
- Are you laughing often and looking in your eyes with love at the face staring back at you?
- Are you being your true self, both inward and outward?
- Are you spending time with people who make you feel good and limiting time spent with people who don't?
- Are you forgiving yourself for what you have perceived you have done wrong?
- Are you accepting yourself the way you are?

- Are you spending regular time having fun? And, if not, what would you like to do?
- Are you finding the joys that are all around you?
- Are you allowing yourself to let your body feel good? Allowing it to feel strong and powerful?
- Are you celebrating the small victories?
- Are you having fun and playing?
- Are you living in gratitude?
- Are you respecting your body and treating it well?
- Are you taking time to be in nature alone?
- Are you getting massages and giving massages to people you love?

The answers you give here will help you mold your life into what you would like it to be. Think about how you can incorporate more joy, fun, and happiness into your daily life.

Kim's story:

Kim is a client of mine who has worked with me for two years. She is a wife and a mother of two teenage girls and is a hardworking and joyous person. She has one difference from most of us: She is without arms. She was in an accident as a young child that killed her mother and put her in an orphanage in Korea. She was adopted by an American family and raised here. There is nothing she can't do. She drives. She has prosthetic arms that she uses but is so adept with her right foot that she drives with her feet. She also has the most beautiful penmanship, writing with her foot. She is so dexterous on her right side it is astounding. My job then is to keep her balanced on the left side and keep up her flexibility, which is very important to her. I wanted to put Kim in my book because she is such an inspiration to me. I love to challenge her with what her body can do.

Question: If you were to define joy, what would it be?

Kim: "Inner contentment which is not dependent on circumstances."

Q: What happens when you are aware that joy is missing?

Kim: "It usually happens after I've gone through a low point in my life, wondering why I feel terrible/depressed, and then it hits me: I haven't been experiencing joy in my life."

Q: How do you identify the missing pieces of joy and bring them in?

Kim: "I have to realize what I am doing to myself and come back to 'reality' and refocus on all of the positives in my life."

Q: Did you have a pivotal moment in your life when you chose joy?

Kim: "I can't think of one moment. I feel like I was taught/grew up with that."

Q: Have you found what takes you out of joy?

Kim: "When I begin comparing my life, kids, and marriage to others' and think it's not enough."

Q: Do you have a practice that keeps you in joy?

Kim: "I have a spiritual life, and that and remembering God's love for me keep me focused."

Step 7: Private Dance Party

The purpose of this next exercise is for you to explore your movement within your own private space. You've heard the quote, "Dance as if no one is watching." Well, do just that. Be in your own space somewhere and crank up the music. You are alone, so move to the music with free abandon, not worrying about anyone else. Don't look over your shoulder, just move.

Put on some music that moves you and just stand in the middle of the room. Close your eyes and allow yourself to move into the music. That is different that dancing to music; it is allowing the music to move through your body, and when it does, movement follows. Keep your eyes closed; that allows you to feel freer, permitting your body to express itself. This is something we rarely give time to—moving.

For me personally, it allows me to open up and see the world in a much clearer way; it is an expression of my life. I have always danced, and it gives me great joy. Put on music and watch children move. They don't care; they can become crazy if the music is just right for them. Not everyone likes to move. If you are self-conscious about your body and if someone told you that you weren't a good dancer, you probably don't like to move very much. Who cares! Try it anyway! What someone told you years ago doesn't have to define the way you move or like to move today. Give it a few times, switch up the music to different styles, and allow your body to move in new and more expansive ways.

The silliness feelings will come up at first, and that's fine; just go with it and try something new. I can see all the men rolling their eyes. Come on try it, or be open to it. Do it by yourself, and after you relax, you will begin to see a freedom in your movement. That's what we are looking for: freedom from our brain stopping us in our flow of expression of movement. Music can move us in an unexpected way, taking us out of our heads and moving us into our hearts. Listen to the music, and let it fill your soul.

Start off with ten to twenty minutes of free movement. Allow your body to move and just keep moving. Put on your favorite Pandora, Spotify, or Apple music station. Let yourself move. Ten minutes is a long time if you have never done it before. Have some water close by for a break, and continue to move. You might feel sore the next day and be very surprised. Don't be. When we move our bodies in unexpected ways, we might feel it in our backs or legs. Warm up and let yourself move and stretch. Start off easy if you haven't danced in a long time. Enjoy the process of being silly, sexy, or crazy.

Recap Chapter 7

The Gateway

1. Being passionate about your life is the new sexy.
2. Most of what we experience is through our physical bodies, but we deal with the world through our feelings.
3. How can we live in a more sensual way in the world? That means dealing with our senses— touch, taste, smell, hearing, and feeling. How do we feel in our skin and in our bodies?
4. Answer all the questions about what you want out of your life in chapter 7.
5. Throw yourself a private dance party. Put on music you love and dance like no one is watching.

Chapter 8

The Reveal

We really don't value our joys. They are taken for granted. There are joys in your life, every minute of the day. That's what I truly believe and live from.

I was talking at an event in Westlake, California, where I was beginning my conversations on joy. After I sat down, the man behind me tapped my shoulder and told me what JOY was an acronym of for him: Jubilant Outpouring of Youthfulness. His name is Joe La Salle, and he told me I could use it. So here it is, Joe, and I thank you for sharing it with me.

I think that's how we fall into our new lives with *joy*. We fall into it because we can find no other way to be. We are tired of living without for so long; there must be something better. We are looking for something. We don't know what we need, but we need a difference. A different feeling that can show up and is waiting to show up in our lives. A change for the better or a change for us.

To become our own cheerleader. Remember, pleasure is always derived from something outside you, whereas joy arises from within.

I had to include in these pages my friend, client, and an amazing woman, Dr. Anna Guanche. She is a board-certified dermatologist and dermatologic surgeon who specializes in procedures that have minimal downtime, such as Ultherapy for skin tightening, CoolSculpting for fat reduction, Fraxel for resurfacing, and other techniques that address specific skin concerns and deliver excellent results.

I asked Dr. Guanche to answer the question, "What is real beauty?"

Here is her response:

> Real beauty is when the inner person is confident, loving of themselves, and fulfilled to the degree that they are ready with something to offer. External beauty complements inner beauty, as it shines through. Empowerment to do a few things to look one's best is part of beauty.

> This is a kind of practice that, like exercise, great diet, and self-care, allows the external shell to look as the inside feels. This is not the desperate, self-absorbed, unhappy, cloying desire to look better

in the hopes of finding happiness; that is a completely different pursuit that does not lead to beauty, but instead to a facade.

I had to ask Dr. Guanche my questions about joy and how she would describe it.

Question: If you were to define joy, what would it be?

Dr. Guanche: "Joy is an inner space of balance and peace. It is a state of effortless, unshakeable well-being."

Q: What happens when you are aware that joy is missing?

Dr. Guanche: "When joy is missing, there is a void or a sense of need and urgency. I understand and acknowledge the feeling. I feel the feeling, which is some form of emotional pain. I realize that this feeling will not cause me to perish. I need not run away from it, but I can feel it, process it, and let it go (rather than fight it or run from it or store it for later). After the moment passes, I find a shift helpful. A favorite song, a belly rub for one of the dogs, a phone call to my best friend, or a positive action or good deed can shift the energy and bring me back to balance/joy."

Q: How do you identify the missing pieces of joy and bring them in?

Dr. Guanche: "I am not looking for the missing pieces. I am looking for joy. In general, I am a joy magnet and surround myself with endeavors, people, art, media, and thoughts that bring me joy. I may become aware that something sad or maddening has happened, but I don't see it as happening *to* me. It is happening. If there is joy missing, so to speak, I redirect my attention or resolve to acquire missing pieces with a steady flow of action and intention toward that goal."

Q: Did you ever have a pivotal moment in your life when you chose joy?

Dr. Guanche: "There was a time when I was complaining. I was unhappy at my job, and I was looking to make a change but had fear and anxiety about starting my own practice. I was listening to business and marketing books on CD with the goal of learning. Quite accidentally, I bought the series *The Power of Now* by Eckhart Tolle, thinking it was a book on efficiency. It taught me about joy, as well as other things, including the law of attraction. It was a pivotal moment in my life. I listened to the series incessantly, and the results have been phenomenal."

Q: Have you found what takes you out of joy?

Dr. Guanche: "Certain input, such as negative news stories or gossip, people who interrupt flow, which is hard to describe, but people who block conversation or force/try to control situations and conversations rather than allowing a flow back and forth, an exchange, take me out of joy. I am better and better at not engaging or maneuvering to avoid these situations when possible. I carefully choose whom to spend time with and what to spend time on. Whatever I give my attention to flourishes, so I actively disengage from individuals who take me out of joy and redouble my efforts to engage with those who do bring me joy and raise my frequency."

Q: Do you have a practice that keeps you in joy?

Dr. Guanche: "I love music. I love to exercise with my favorite music on. I can easily remember lyrics to songs, so I sing often with the radio or in exercise classes. I find joy and laughter and learning in almost every interaction. I am ready to receive love, and I am ready to learn from everyone I interact with. This way no interaction is dull for me."

I am going to add to this that Anna is the most inspiring person to be around. She is uplifting and, most of all, fun. On top of everything else, she is a gorgeous woman and a fantastic doctor. That's whom I want to be around.

You can step into your joy from just noticing how much joy there is for you every day, everywhere, in every moment. Start noticing and looking for it. I've talked about a joy journal where you can start to notice and pay attention to joys that are all around you. Write down every joyous, delicious moment. Look for joy everywhere. It is there waiting for you to notice. "Pick me, pick me," joy says, everywhere we look. Value your life, and your joys will show up, as though a veil has been lifted. Even if you can't see it, make believe it is there. Start writing what you wish to see, and suddenly it will begin to appear. Believe it is there.

All your tools for feeling better are listed below:

1. Breathing
2. Walking meditation
3. Foam roller
4. Letter to your younger self
5. Baths and bodywork
6. Joy journal
7. Dance party

The beautiful movements of the clouds as they cross the sky, seeing someone you love come off the plane at the airport, your first cup of coffee or tea in the morning, a wonderful evening with friends, the first peek of flowers in the spring, the first snow, your first kiss, your last kiss, opening your heart to someone, quiet moments, loud moments filled with crazy fun energy, fearing something and then overcoming that fear, finding your passion, reconnecting with an old friend: It does not have to be a big thing; enjoy and savor the small treats that come your way.

In her *Psychology Today* post referred to in chapter 1, Dr. Seppälä details a study by Nathaniel Lambert and colleagues at Brigham Young University that showed that discussing positive experiences leads to heightened well-being and increased overall life satisfaction and energy. We are reluctant to talk about our good fortune. We don't want to show off. We don't want to feel guilty or, most important, jinx ourselves. We bond with others over complaints, commiserate, and even gossip to feel better. Lambert and his colleagues suggest that describing our happy experiences to our close friends and romantic partners is a better idea. These are people who really care about us and want what's best for us. Making lists of positive things that we are grateful for helps us draw our attention to the positive experiences in life (Seppälä, 2013).

We want to keep ourselves in as high a vibrational level as we can tolerate. I always try to get my clients to notice how far they have come in their physical movement. I have them take themselves back to the time when they started with me, so they can see exercises that are easy for them now but were very challenging before.

Maybe they have been in constant pain, and now the pain is less frequent. They could only walk for ten minutes, and now they are walking for an hour. It is the little victories that take us to the finish line—not the big leap, but all the other little steps that get us to the end. That is why we must notice and celebrate with others around us, not worrying so much about the outcome and sharing in their victories as well, taking in our magnificence every day.

Jayme's story:

Sometimes you make a difference in someone's life, and you don't even know it. That was what happened with my friend Jayme and me. I became the owner of The Absolute & Yoga Studio, and I was excited to share my space with everyone. When I ran into Jayme, she was complaining about feeling crappy and out of shape. I was so excited to share my studio with her. At first she was not really thrilled by the prospect, but I continued to nudge her to come in. She did, and slowly but surely, she started to love to move. She was there almost every day, and it was amazing to see how much she changed. She was happier. It changed her body, how her family ate, and, eventually, her life.

Here is what Jayme said about her experience:

> I've known Conni for a long time; our children went to school together. Last year at the school carnival I was sixty pounds overweight, forty-five years old, and not happy. Conni asked me what was wrong. She let me cry on her shoulder and then suggested I try her studio. "*No thanks!*" I said. "I haven't been inside a gym in over twenty years."
>
> Conni said a studio was not like a gym; it was smaller, more intimate, and with personal teaching. She said, "Just try my Pilates on the ball class." She didn't understand: I didn't need exercise; I needed a whole new life. I put up a fight but finally got there. I started with Pilates mat and dance and really liked Pilates. Conni and her teachers were so encouraging; somehow she makes you think that trying to do the extra challenge was your idea.

Conni has a positive can-do attitude. She has encouraged me to be the best I can be. Now, ten months later, I am down thirty-one pounds, and I have a completely different attitude. I'm still working toward my goal, but I enjoy the process as much as the results.

The only thing that has changed is me. But it feels like everything is different. Who knew a little exercise could do so much? Conni did!

Step 8: Joy Playlist

Most of us have music that we enjoy and playlists we have made. I want you to put on a playlist all your most favorite music that makes you just feel great. This takes a little time and work to pull it all together, but it is well worth the trouble. Think of it as your own joy coach that is pulling for you whenever you need a jolt of *joy*.

Play it often, and keep adding to it. Play it loud, and dance or sing to it. Allow yourself to be full of life and silliness. Do this daily, weekly, or monthly. Keep adding to your list; play it when you need a pick-me-up. Also, think of a song that would be the title for the soundtrack of your life. When you are stuck in a difficult day, put on your playlist and let it send you into a different mood.

Here is a portion of my playlist:

> "Happy" – Pharrell Williams
> "It's Raining Men" – The Weather Girls
> "Home" – Michael Bublé
> "Stay" – Alison Kraus
> "Taking It to the Streets" –
> The Doobie Brothers
> "Fight Song" – Rachel Platten
> "Shut Up and Dance" – Walk the Moon
> "All I Want" – Joni Mitchell
> "You've Got a Friend" – Carole King
> "I Gotta Feeling" – The Black Eyed Peas
> "Keeps Gettin' Better" – Christina Aguliera
> "Tubthumping" – Chumbawamba
> "A Sky Full of Stars" – Coldplay
> "One, Two Step" – Ciara
> "Put Your Records On" – Corinne Bailey Rae
> "Suite: Judy Blue Eyes" – Crosby, Stills &
> Nash
> "100 Years" – Five for Fighting
> "Say It Right" – Nelly Furtado
> "Just the Two of Us" –
> Grover Washington, Jr and Bill Withers
> "At Last" – Etta James
> "I feel good"- James Brown
> "Miami 2017" – Billy Joel

This is just a sampling. I keep adding new music. Some I get from friends, my kids give me new artists, and listening to Pandora helps me find other artists that I love. Let your playlist be the soundtrack for your life. Ever have the experience when you are in traffic and you're a kind of mad and totally frustrated, and then a great song comes on and changes everything up in that moment? You start singing and not caring so much about the traffic. You might even arrive home but sit in the driveway just to finish the song. Those are the songs we want on our lists—the ones that make you so happy you sing at the top of your lungs, and you don't care who's watching you.

I was walking down the street, and a woman drove by me, windows open, singing at the top of her lungs, not a care in the world, and totally in joy. I had to smile, as did everyone else on the street; then we all started to talk to each other. We all were strangers, but her joy was contagious.

Keep adding to your list and collecting from different places. Ask your friends what some of their joy songs are to get a different mix. Keep adding to it and revising your list. The old songs you love, plus the new ones; keep them coming.

We are not our thoughts, feelings, or pains. They are just passing through us; we are the vessel that holds everything. If we can show up with vulnerability, that is the path to more love, connection, and spirit. If we can allow things to move through us and not attach, we get to see a different view of the world. Let's say we get to see the bigger picture. We get to allow ourselves to be in the moment and let life reveal itself to us without attaching too much to any of it: the good, the bad, and the indifferent. In that moment, we are just full of possibilities, to become even greater than what we believed we were. We can have a larger view of the world and an even larger view of what we think our lives are about.

That is what The Reveal is about: We don't have to do or be any different. We need to reveal the magic that lies within all of us. It is in *all* of us in every moment. We just have to move from one moment to the next, well aware that the next moment always comes. So if you are in a difficult place, at some point it will move past you. Even the most beautiful moment moves past you. That's how it works and why we want to live in the moment— why we want to be mindful. If we aren't, we may miss the beautiful moment. But no worries, another one will come along. I think of all the beautiful moments when I wasn't paying attention—moments I missed with my parents, my brothers growing up, grandparents, cousins, friends, my husband, and my children. I want to stay conscious so I don't miss my life. It goes by fast enough even when we are paying attention.

I know you feel the same way I do, so start to pay attention to your own life and where it is taking you and how you feel and who is in your life with you. Choose the better feelings over the weaker ones; choose good friends over the ones who don't really care about you; choose *your* life first. Everything else will fall into place.

Recap Chapter 8

The Reveal

1. JOY acronym: Jubilant Outpouring of Youthfulness
2. Look around you and notice the evidence of joy all around you.
3. We are reluctant to discuss our positive feelings because we are afraid they will disappear if we talk about them.
4. We are everything we are looking for.
5. Joy playlist: Keep all the music in one place that makes you feel good and alive. Keep adding to it. It's the music that you want to sing at the top of your lungs. When you are down, it perks you right up.

Falling into Joy: The End of My Story, for Now

Here it is a beautiful holiday morning. It is quiet, the birds are chirping, and the light is slowly creeping into the sky. I love early morning—the unexpected delight of limitless possibilities. Here I am at the end of my story, and since I've started my journey writing about joy, the most unjoyful events have happened. Lots of anger and impatience with myself and those around me. Lots of family drama, kids not doing what I want them to, my daughter needing surgery on her leg, going through the surgery with her and worrying, and then helping her deal with the pain and getting better, not taking care of my body or my needs, stressing out and being unkind, one kid going to college and one kid coming out of college, and all the stresses that brings in my kids' lives, letting myself get into debt over my business because I didn't want to let others down, my father's death, letting my concerns for others become more important than me. I think the final straw was the day I was at the drive-through at Starbucks. I was at the proper distance from the car in front of me because there was a giant X indicating a no-standing zone, and I know you are not supposed to be in that giant X. A woman pulled right in front of me, as if I weren't there. I started honking my horn and, frankly, going kind of crazy.

As she waited in the line to order her coffee, I wanted to jump out and yell at her and create a scene, as I got more and more upset by it all. Instead, I started just yelling and screaming in my car. I never do that, but I was over-the-top crazy. I looked at myself in the rearview mirror, saw how crazy I was, and started laughing at myself. I just started to fill with total hysteria about me and going that crazy over coffee or someone cutting in line. Really? I was getting so upset over what? Was it really the woman, or was it that I didn't pull up close to the car in front of me? Did I have to listen to the rules?

It really had nothing to do with her and everything to do with me. I am a good girl, I follow the rules, and I do what I'm supposed to. And that was the problem. Sometimes it doesn't work out. That is the way it goes, and guess what? You still can be joyous! We all just need to value what's around us and mostly what's in us. End of story.

We need to stop being so hard on ourselves for the things that didn't happen and understand that sometimes in getting what we think we don't want we get what we need. We can only see all of it by looking back, and believe me, it seems to all work out. We need to give ourselves the time to have space and time to take care of our bodies. When we have done that, everything begins to change.

Miracles are all around us. We just don't open our eyes enough to see them. It's the same with joy. We don't allow ourselves the time to see it and take it in. That ultimately leads from joy into peace. And, really, isn't that what we want in our lives? Joy, then peace.

This all became so clear to me being in the hospital with my daughter. She was really surrounded by angels, every one of them helping in whatever capacity they fulfilled: helping with pain, explaining the surgery, showing kindness. Some people screaming in pain were all alone, but my daughter, my husband, and I decided together to look at the whole experience differently, and all we saw was the love and support surrounding us. And all we felt in return was love and support for those angels, from the cleaning crew up to the doctors.

We love; we lose; we lose friends and family, and we find new friends and family; we move and leave old friends behind only to discover new ones; we leave old friends only to discover that we can go back, and those old friends are still there, waiting to hear our stories and share in our lives, just as we are willing to listen and share with them. We win, we lose, we succeed, we fail; there is birth and death; we shut our hearts down, and hopefully, we break them wide open, contracting and expanding. That is the energy of life. Like jellyfish, we propel ourselves through the ocean of life, constantly moving and changing, sometimes knowing where we are going, and many times just being pushed around by the currents. All we need to know is that at the bottom of it all we will be okay.

I hope that maybe you saw yourself in the different case studies or could connect in some way with a part of my story. The exercises are for you to do. Don't just think about them; incorporate them into your lives. I kept them simple and easy to do anywhere. Breathing, walking meditation, foam roller, letter to your younger self, joy diary, dance party, baths, joy playlist—all of them allow you to focus on yourself. What they say in the airplane is true: Put your mask on first and then help someone else. Do this. Allow yourself to be the center of your life. Don't let everyone else in your life steal your time. Fight for you. Fight for the time to take care of yourself. Quiet time, rest time, breathing room, time to exercise, play, be silly, and be loud—whatever it is that you need. Put yourself in the front of the line.

In the end, we have ourselves, and we need to let in the sadness, so we can feel the joy—the joy of air going into our lungs another day on this unbelievable planet, having that first cup of coffee, or feeling the connection with another human being. All of it should be treated with great reverence and love.

Why should joy matter? Because it is our right to have a life filled with heart-opened wonder and joy.

Being passionate about what you do in the world and feeling like you are part of this planet matters. It matters to feel that you want to connect with people and that your connection makes a difference and makes the world just a little bit better because you are here.

I want to leave my footprint in as many places as I can and to connect with as many people as I can and have a deep and meaningful connection.

I needed to go back to my hometown to my high school reunion, because I believe the people you grew up with are in your DNA. They are part of the fibers that make up who you are. I know lots of people who don't like to go back home again, but I feel I needed that to move forward and see who I was so I could appreciate the woman I had become.

I got to spend the weekend with the woman who was my best friend growing up and her husband. I sat for an entire afternoon with Corin Basilion on a pond in October, looking out over the beautiful fall foliage in Glen Cove, Long Island, and we talked about our lives now, reminisced about growing up together, and spoke of our children and husbands—just like all the times we talked when we were younger and had dreams of our future.

Sitting with a friend you have known for fifty years is quite moving; it gives substance to your life and validation to all the crazy twists and turns your life has taken. You leave those things behind and know there is someone else out there who has your back; time and space do not change that friendship. It is coming full circle to go back to the place where you felt you had to run away from and wanted nothing to do with. I had to leave and grow and change in order to come back. I think you only get that understanding from getting older and letting that change you.

That's what I wish for your life: that you step into it, love it, embrace it, protect it, and make sure that when you leave you have left a footprint somewhere and everywhere. Above all, let joy move you forward. In the end, all that matters is your breath. Take a deep breath in, and exhale slowly on the rest of your life.

Joy is the juice of life freshly squeezed. How will you drink it in?

Conni Ponturo

Acknowledgements

A deep thank you to Marsh Engle who started me on my journey as a writer and kept me forging ahead. Donald Berman whose insightful edits kept me on track both with grammar and with content. Michael Hacker for formatting. A big thank you to Balboa Press for all their help. Genine Smith for her fabulous cover and back design. Kathy Rapport for my book photo; To my mother who gave me a joyful heart, and my father who's love of life was contagious. My three brothers, Dick, Bob, and Doug, for supporting me and being wonderful brothers and my beautiful sisters in laws for being with them. My group of girlfriends who keep me in touch with why I am here: Anne Howard, Michelle Stone, Maria Leone, Randa Haffar, Monika Hall, Julie Rowlands, Diane Delaney, Electra Manwiller, Jill Heilmer, and Corin Basilion. To my clients, Jay, Bruce, Tanya, and Jayme, who generously allowed me use their stories. To John Vosler, Anne Howard, Lori Shayew, Tanna Marshall, Kim Flanagan, and Dr. Anna Guanche for taking their time to thoughtfully answer my questions on joy. And to all of the fantastic clients that have graced my doors over the years thank you, this book would not exist without you.

References

Brown, Brené. 2012. *Daring Greatly: How the Courage to Be Vulnerable Transforms the Way We Live, Love, Parent, and Lead*. New York: Penguin Random House.

Campbell, J. (1949). *The hero with a thousand faces*. Novato, CA: New World Library.

Cooper, B. (2013, November 13). The science behind posture and how it affects your brain [Web log post]. Retrieved from http://lifehacker.com/the-science-behind-posture-and-how-it-affects-your-brain-1463291618

Cuddy, Amy. 2012. "Your Body Language Shapes Who You Are" (speech). Retrieved from https://www.ted.com/talks/amy_cuddy_your_body_language_shapes_who_you_are?language=en

Dyer, Wayne. 2012. *Wishes Fulfilled: The Art of Manifesting*. Carlsbad, CA: Hay House, Inc.

Gable, Shelley and Jonathan Haidt. 2005. "What (and Why) Is Positive Psychology." *Review of General Psychology*, *9*(2), 103–110.

Seppälä, Emma. 2013. "The Science behind the Joy of Sharing Joy." Retrieved from https://www.psychologytoday.com/blog/feeling-it/201307/the-science-behind-the-joy-sharing-joy

Williamson, Marianne. 1992. *A Return to Love: Reflections on the Principles of a Course in Miracles*. New York: Harper Collins.

Printed in the United States
By Bookmasters